The Indispensable CALVIN AND HOBBES

A Calvin and Hobbes Treasury by

BILL WATTERSON

Includes cartoons from *The Revenge of the Baby-Sat* and *Scientific Progress Goes "Boink"*

Andrews and McMeel ▪ A Universal Press Syndicate Company ▪ Kansas City

Calvin and Hobbes is distributed internationally by Universal Press Syndicate.

ISBN: 0-8362-1898-1 (paperback)
0-8362-1703-9 (hardback)

Library of Congress Catalog Card Number: 92-72247 (paperback)
92-72248 (hardback)

I made a big decision a little while ago.
I don't remember what it was, which prob'ly goes to show
That many times a simple choice can prove to be essential
Even though it often might appear inconsequential.

I must have been distracted when I left my home because
Left or right I'm sure I went. (I wonder which it was!)
Anyway, I never veered: I walked in that direction
Utterly absorbed, it seems, in quiet introspection.

For no reason I can think of, I've wandered far astray.
And that is how I got to where I find myself today.

Explorers are we, intrepid and bold,
Out in the wild, amongst wonders untold.
Equipped with our wits, a map, and a snack,
We're searching for fun and we're on the right track!

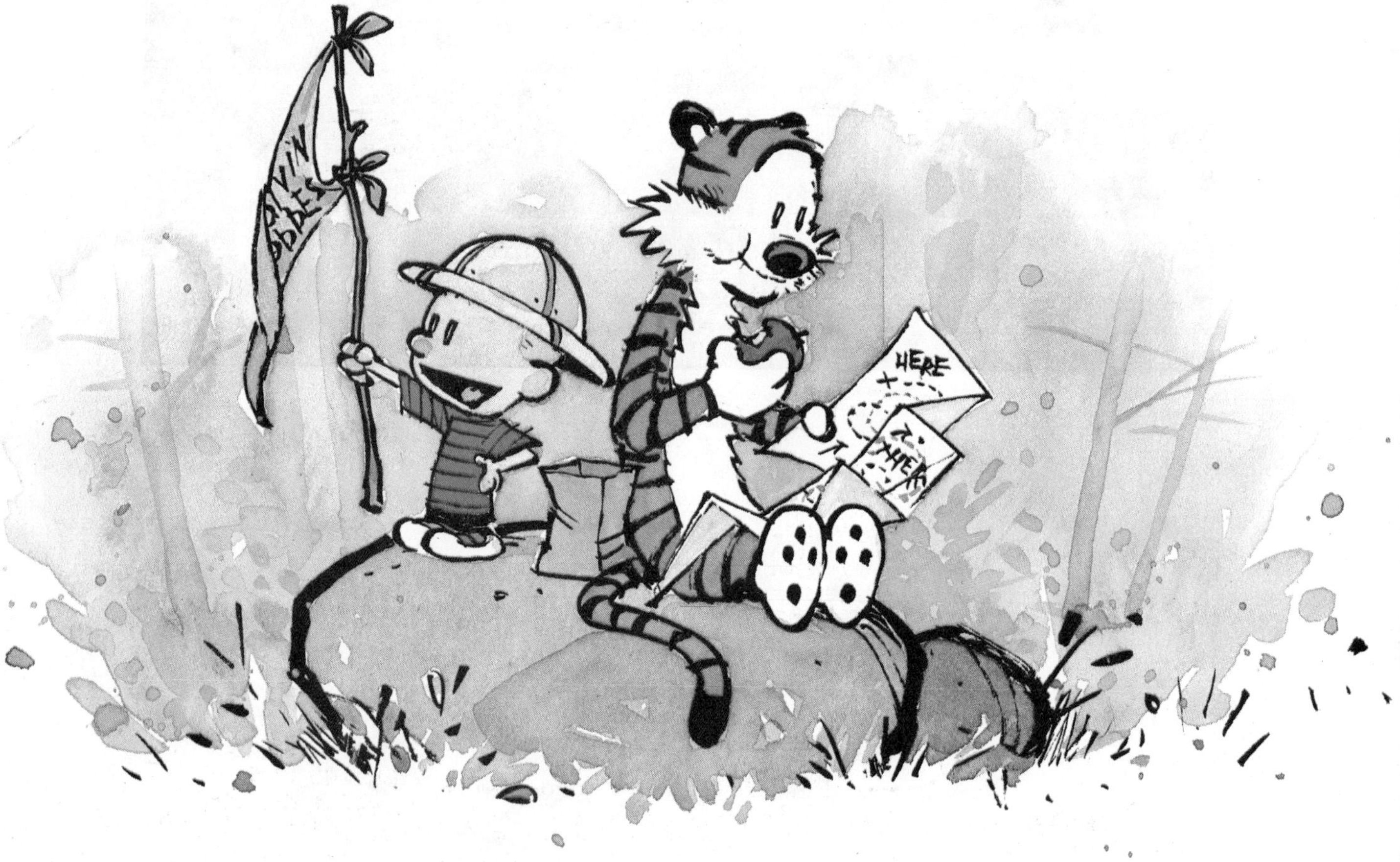
HERE

My mother has eyes on the back of her head!
I don't quite believe it, but that's what she said.
She explained that she'd been so uniquely endowed
To catch me when I did Things Not Allowed.
I think she must also have eyes on her rear.
I've noticed her hindsight is unusually clear.

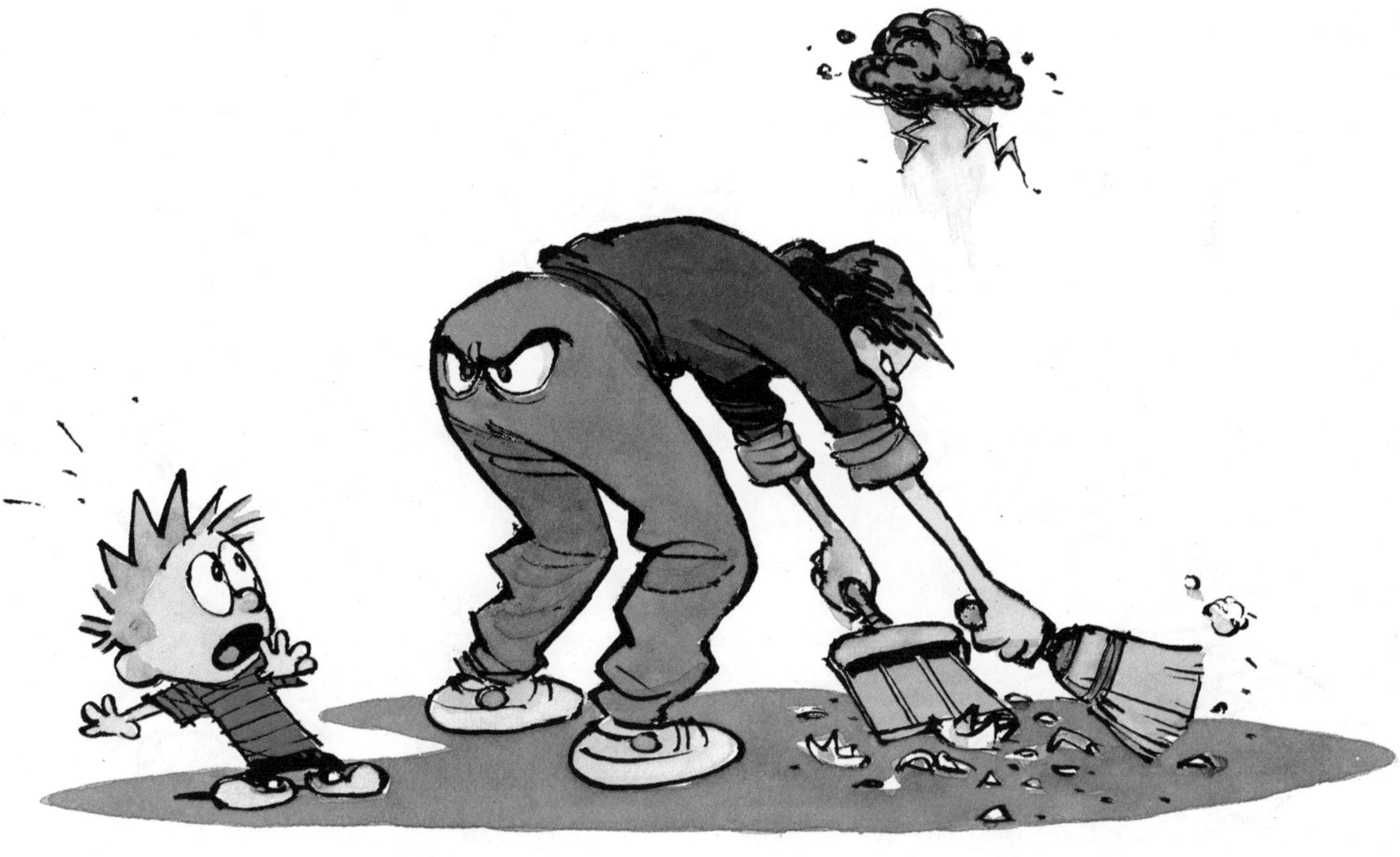

At night my mind does not much care
If what it thinks is here or there.
It tells me stories it invents
And makes up things that don't make sense.
I don't know why it does this stuff.
The real world seems quite weird enough.

What if my bones were in a museum,
Where aliens paid good money to see 'em?
And suppose that they'd put me together all wrong,
Sticking bones on to bones where they didn't belong!

Imagine phalanges, pelvis, and spine
Welded to mandibles that once had been mine!
With each misassemblage, the error compounded,
The aliens would draw back in terror, astounded!

Their textbooks would show me in grim illustration,
The most hideous thing ever seen in creation!
The museum would commission a model in plaster
Of ME, to be called, "Evolution's Disaster"!

And paleontologists there would debate
Dozens of theories to help postulate
How man survived for those thousands of years
With teeth-covered arms growing out of his ears!

Oh, I hope that I'm never in such manner displayed,
No matter HOW much to see me the aliens paid.

I did not want to go with them.
Alas, I had no choice.
This was made quite clear to me
In threat'ning tones of voice.

I protested mightily
And scrambled 'cross the floor.
But though I grabbed the furniture,
They dragged me out the door.

In the car, I screamed and moaned.
I cried my red eyes dry.
The window down, I yelled for help
To people we passed by.

Mom and Dad can make the rules
And certain things forbid,
But I can make them wish that they
Had never had a kid.

Now I'm in bed,
The sheets pulled to my head.
My tiger is here making Zs.
He's furry and hot.
He takes up a lot
Of the bed and he's hogging the breeze.

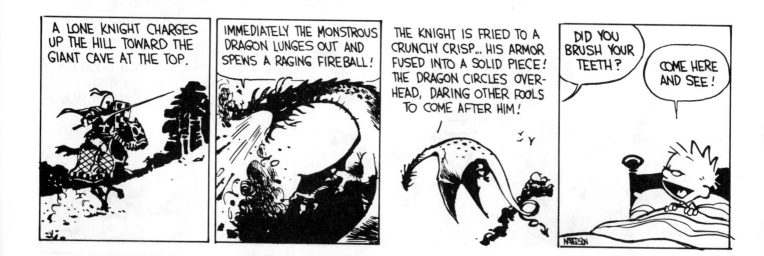

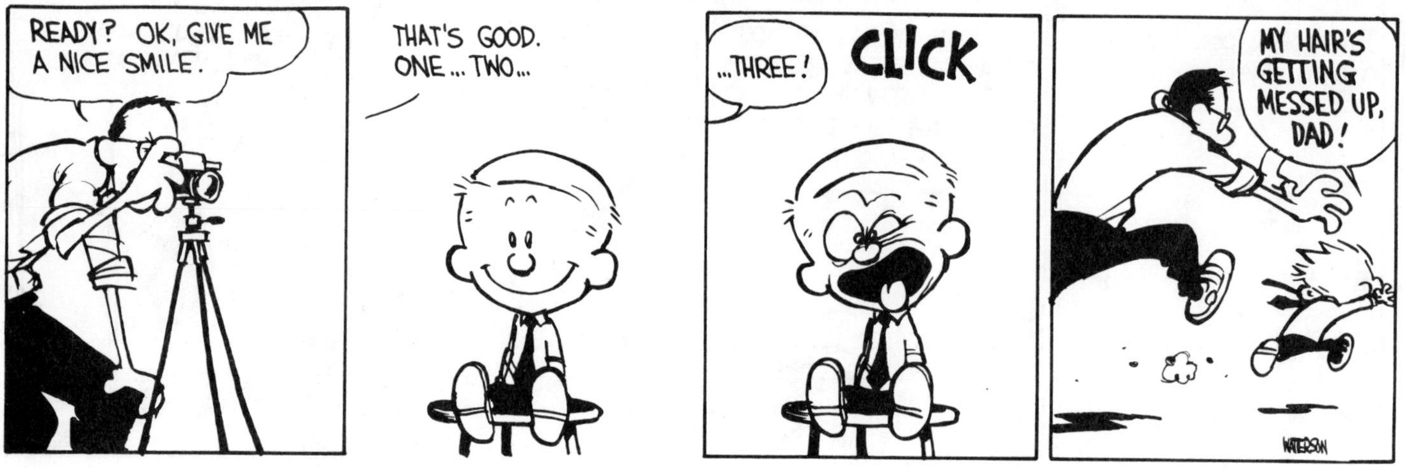
READY? OK, GIVE ME A NICE SMILE.
THAT'S GOOD. ONE... TWO...
...THREE!
CLICK
MY HAIR'S GETTING MESSED UP, DAD!

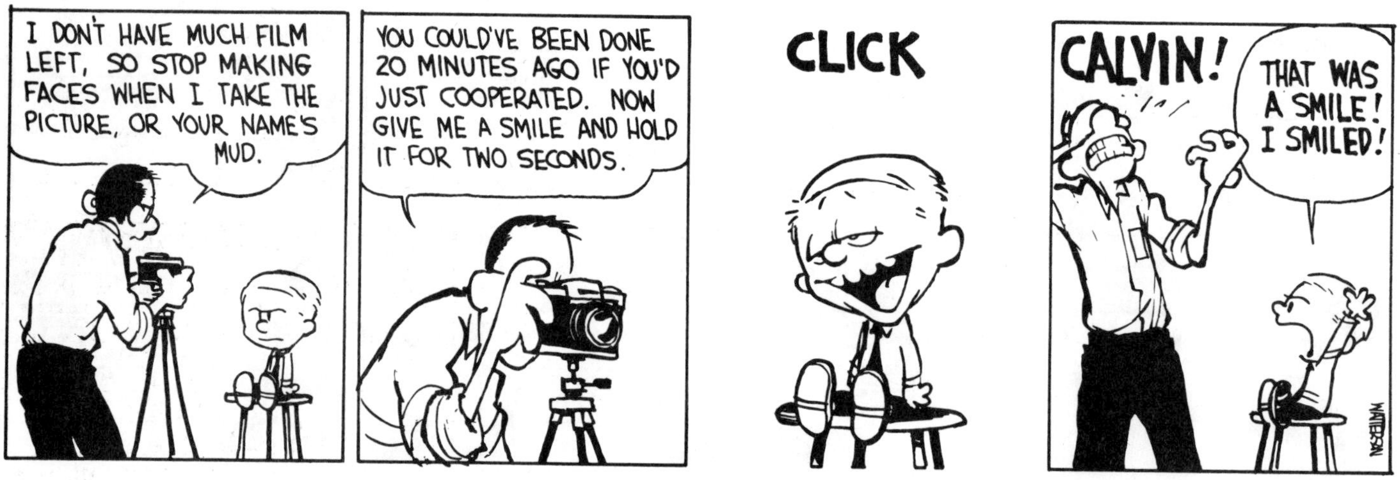
I DON'T HAVE MUCH FILM LEFT, SO STOP MAKING FACES WHEN I TAKE THE PICTURE, OR YOUR NAME'S MUD.
YOU COULD'VE BEEN DONE 20 MINUTES AGO IF YOU'D JUST COOPERATED. NOW GIVE ME A SMILE AND HOLD IT FOR TWO SECONDS.
CLICK
CALVIN!
THAT WAS A SMILE! I SMILED!

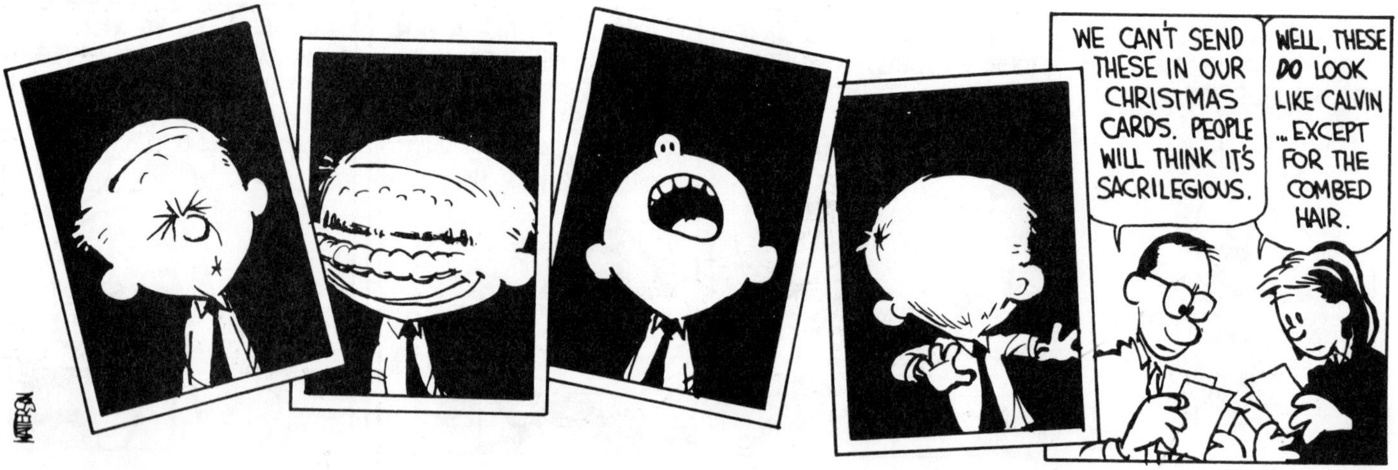
WE CAN'T SEND THESE IN OUR CHRISTMAS CARDS. PEOPLE WILL THINK IT'S SACRILEGIOUS.
WELL, THESE **DO** LOOK LIKE CALVIN ... EXCEPT FOR THE COMBED HAIR.

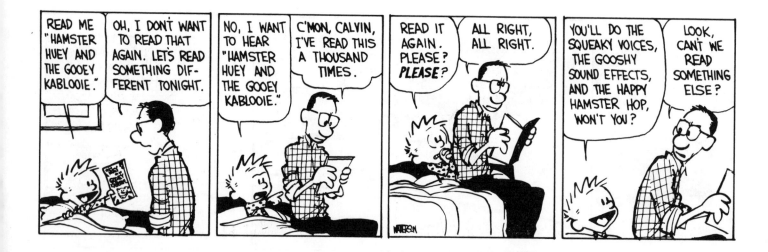

YES, CAN I HAVE THE TOOL DEPARTMENT, PLEASE? THANK YOU.

HELLO? HOW MUCH ARE YOUR POWER CIRCULAR SAWS? I SEE. AND YOUR ELECTRIC DRILLS? UH-HUH. HOW BIG OF A BIT WILL THAT HOLD? REALLY? GREAT.

SO THE ASSIGNMENT IS PAGES TWO THROUGH FOUR? OK, THANKS SUSIE.

..SORRY ABOUT THAT. DO YOU CARRY ACETYLENE TORCHES? OK, RING IT ALL UP. THIS WILL BE ON MASTERCARD.

LOOK AT ALL THIS HOMEWORK I'M SUPPOSED TO DO!

I DON'T WANT TO DO THIS GARBAGE! I WANT TO GO PLAY OUTSIDE!

CHILDHOOD IS SHORT AND MATURITY IS FOREVER.

PEOPLE ARE ROTTEN.

WHEN I GROW UP, I'M GOING TO LIVE A MILLION MILES AWAY FROM EVERYONE!

HOW WILL YOU SURVIVE? WHAT WILL YOU EAT?

...WELL, MOM COULD COME BY TWICE A DAY TO COOK, I SUPPOSE.

THAT WOULD BE QUITE A COMMUTE.

GET A LOAD OF *THIS* DUMB ASSIGNMENT! I'M SUPPOSED TO WRITE ABOUT AN ADVENTURE I'VE HAD!

I HAVEN'T HAD ANY ADVENTURES! MY LIFE HAS BEEN ONE BIG BORE FROM THE BEGINNING!

HAVE I EVER BEEN ABDUCTED BY PIRATES? HAVE I EVER FACED DOWN A CHARGING RHINO? HAVE I EVER BEEN IN A SHOOT-OUT, OR ON A BOMBING RAID? **NO!** I NEVER GET TO HAVE ADVENTURES!

WHAT ABOUT THE TIME YOU BACKED THE CAR THROUGH THE GARAGE DOOR?

YOU CALL THAT AN ADVENTURE? I DIDN'T EVEN GET ON THE HIGHWAY.

WHEN DO YOU THINK WE'LL GET A THUNDER AND LIGHTNING STORM?

I DON'T KNOW. PROBABLY NOT UNTIL SPRING.

I THINK HE'S GOING TO MELT BEFORE WE CAN BRING HIM TO LIFE.

HEY, SUSIE, STAND ON THIS "X."

WHY?

NO REASON. JUST DO IT. I DARE YOU.

NO.

PLEASE? C'MON!

GET LOST.

THIS MAY NOT WORK OUT AS WELL AS I THOUGHT.

43

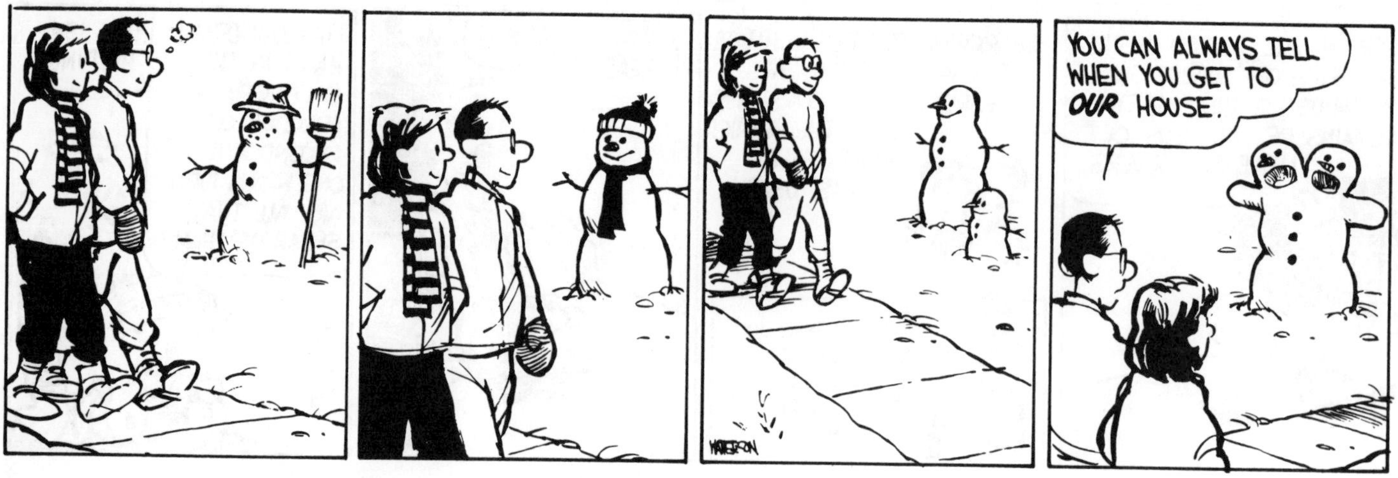
YOU CAN ALWAYS TELL WHEN YOU GET TO **OUR** HOUSE.

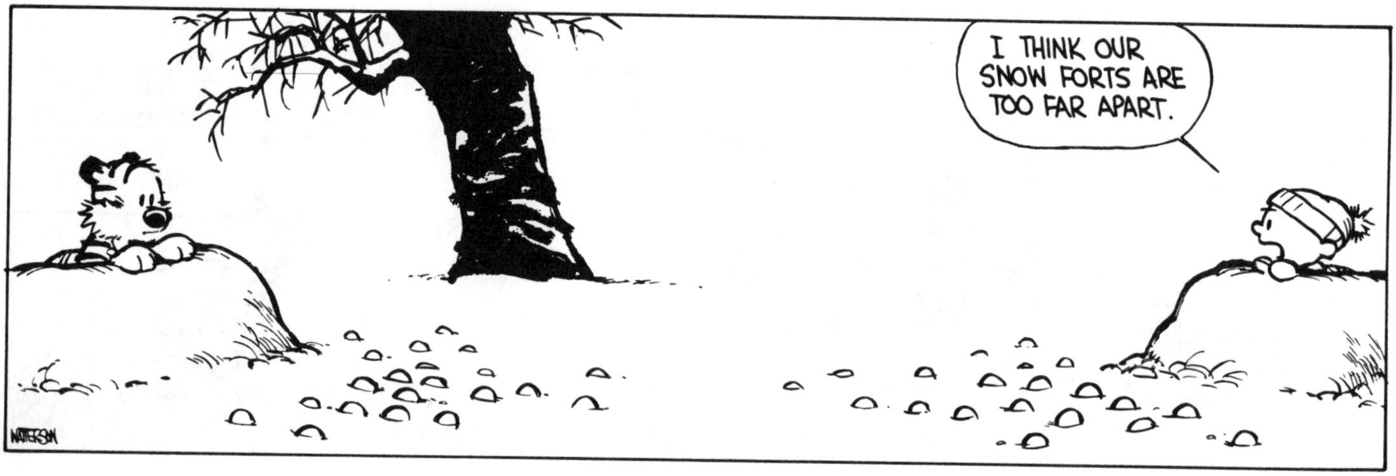
I THINK OUR SNOW FORTS ARE TOO FAR APART.

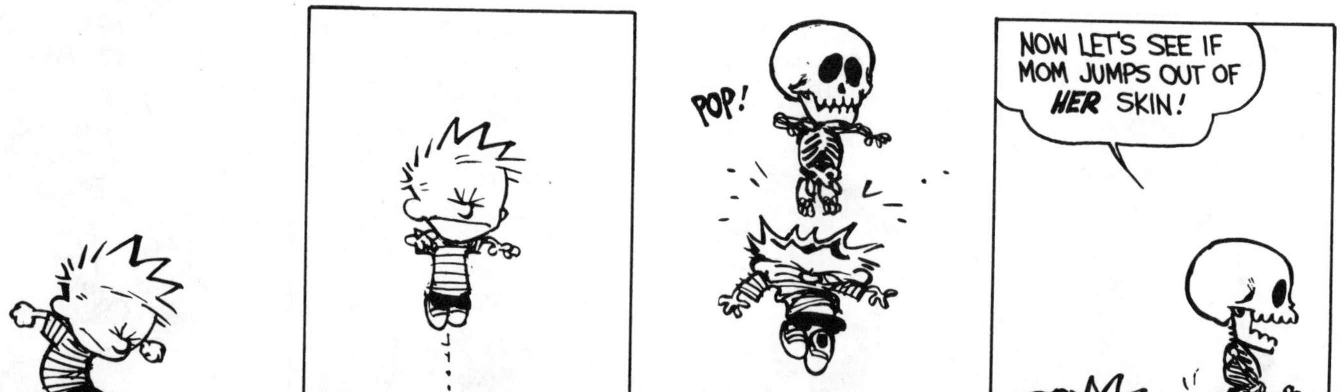
POP!
NOW LET'S SEE IF MOM JUMPS OUT OF **HER** SKIN!

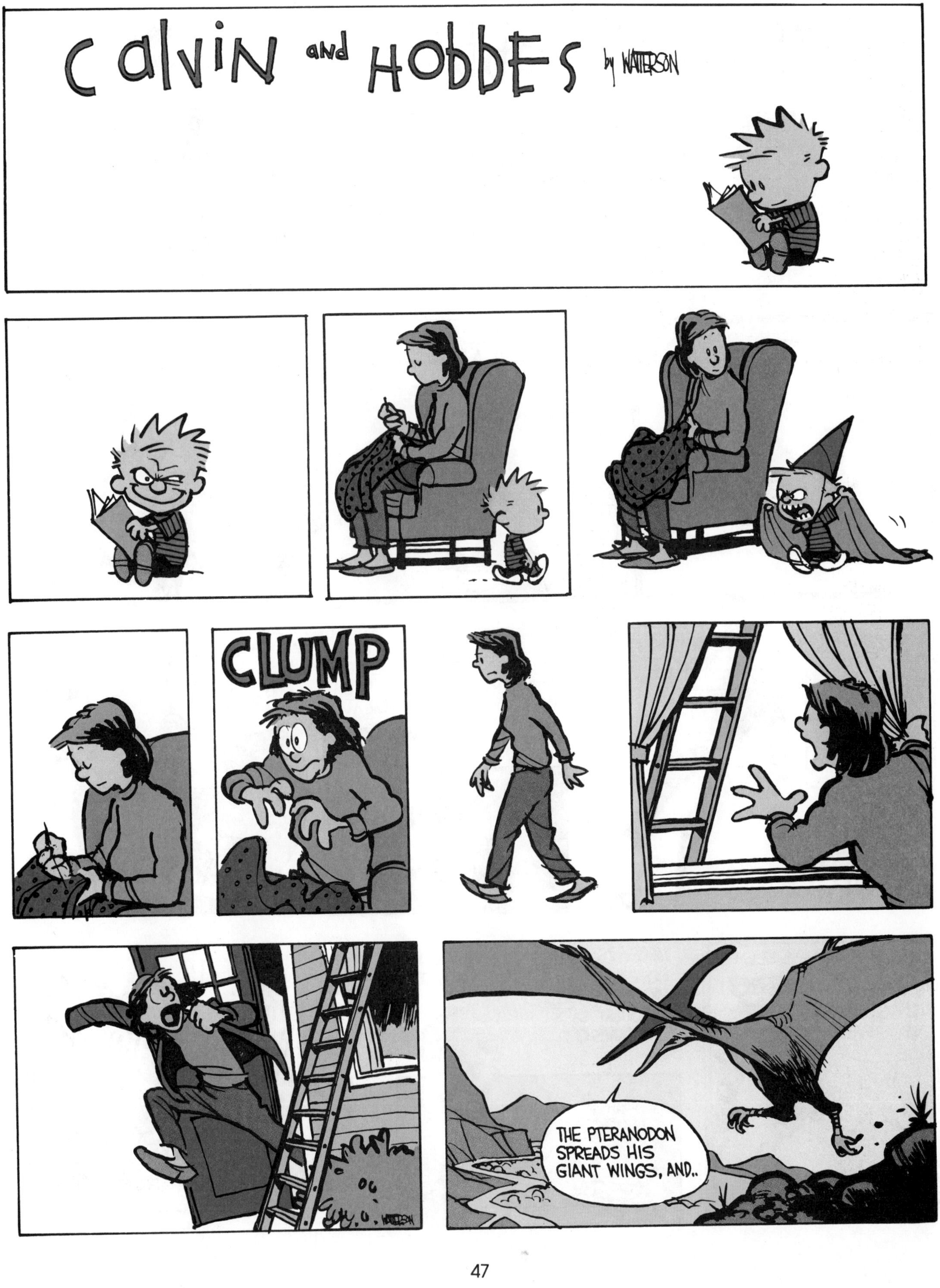
Calvin and HOBBES by WATTERSON
CLUMP
THE PTERANODON SPREADS HIS GIANT WINGS, AND..
WATTERSON

49

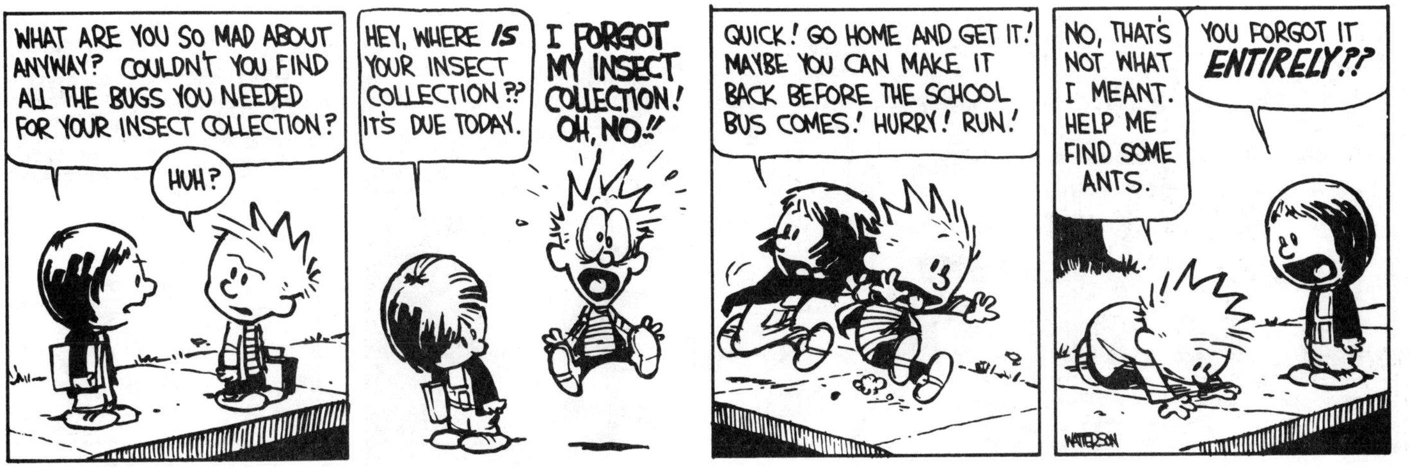
WHAT ARE YOU SO MAD ABOUT ANYWAY? COULDN'T YOU FIND ALL THE BUGS YOU NEEDED FOR YOUR INSECT COLLECTION?
HUH?
HEY, WHERE *IS* YOUR INSECT COLLECTION?? IT'S DUE TODAY.
I FORGOT MY INSECT COLLECTION! OH, NO!!
QUICK! GO HOME AND GET IT! MAYBE YOU CAN MAKE IT BACK BEFORE THE SCHOOL BUS COMES! HURRY! RUN!
NO, THAT'S NOT WHAT I MEANT. HELP ME FIND SOME ANTS.
YOU FORGOT IT *ENTIRELY*??
WATTERSON

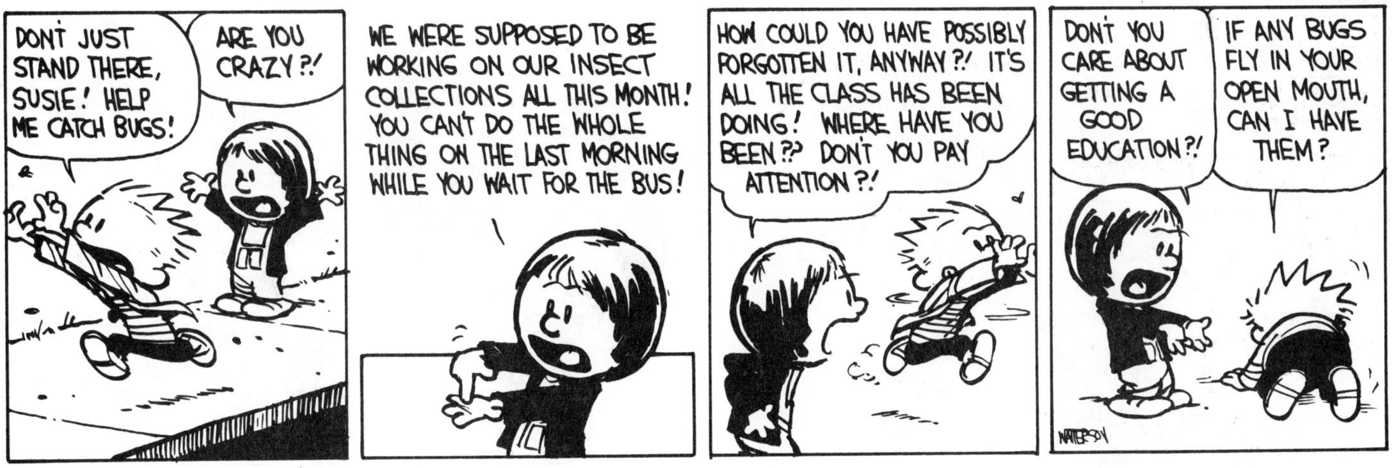
DON'T JUST STAND THERE, SUSIE! HELP ME CATCH BUGS!
ARE YOU CRAZY?!
WE WERE SUPPOSED TO BE WORKING ON OUR INSECT COLLECTIONS ALL THIS MONTH! YOU CAN'T DO THE WHOLE THING ON THE LAST MORNING WHILE YOU WAIT FOR THE BUS!
HOW COULD YOU HAVE POSSIBLY FORGOTTEN IT, ANYWAY?! IT'S ALL THE CLASS HAS BEEN DOING! WHERE HAVE YOU BEEN?? DON'T YOU PAY ATTENTION?!
DON'T YOU CARE ABOUT GETTING A GOOD EDUCATION?!
IF ANY BUGS FLY IN YOUR OPEN MOUTH, CAN I HAVE THEM?
WATTERSON

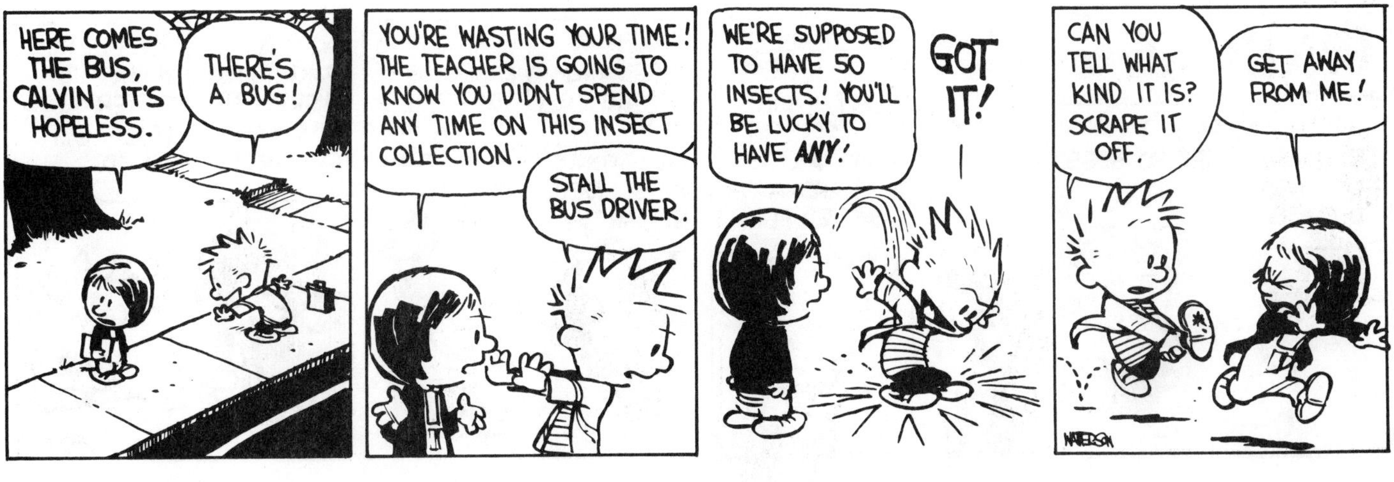
HERE COMES THE BUS, CALVIN. IT'S HOPELESS.
THERE'S A BUG!
YOU'RE WASTING YOUR TIME! THE TEACHER IS GOING TO KNOW YOU DIDN'T SPEND ANY TIME ON THIS INSECT COLLECTION.
STALL THE BUS DRIVER.
WE'RE SUPPOSED TO HAVE 50 INSECTS! YOU'LL BE LUCKY TO HAVE *ANY*!
GOT IT!
CAN YOU TELL WHAT KIND IT IS? SCRAPE IT OFF.
GET AWAY FROM ME!
WATTERSON

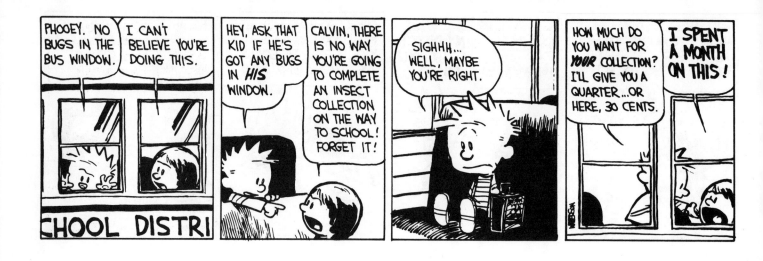

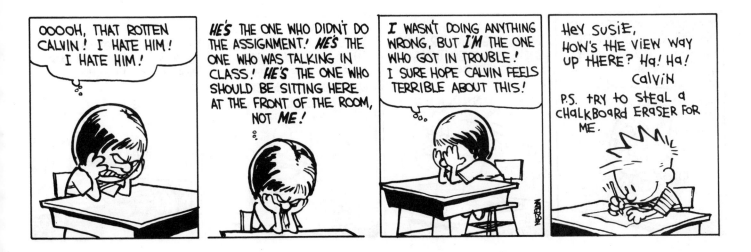

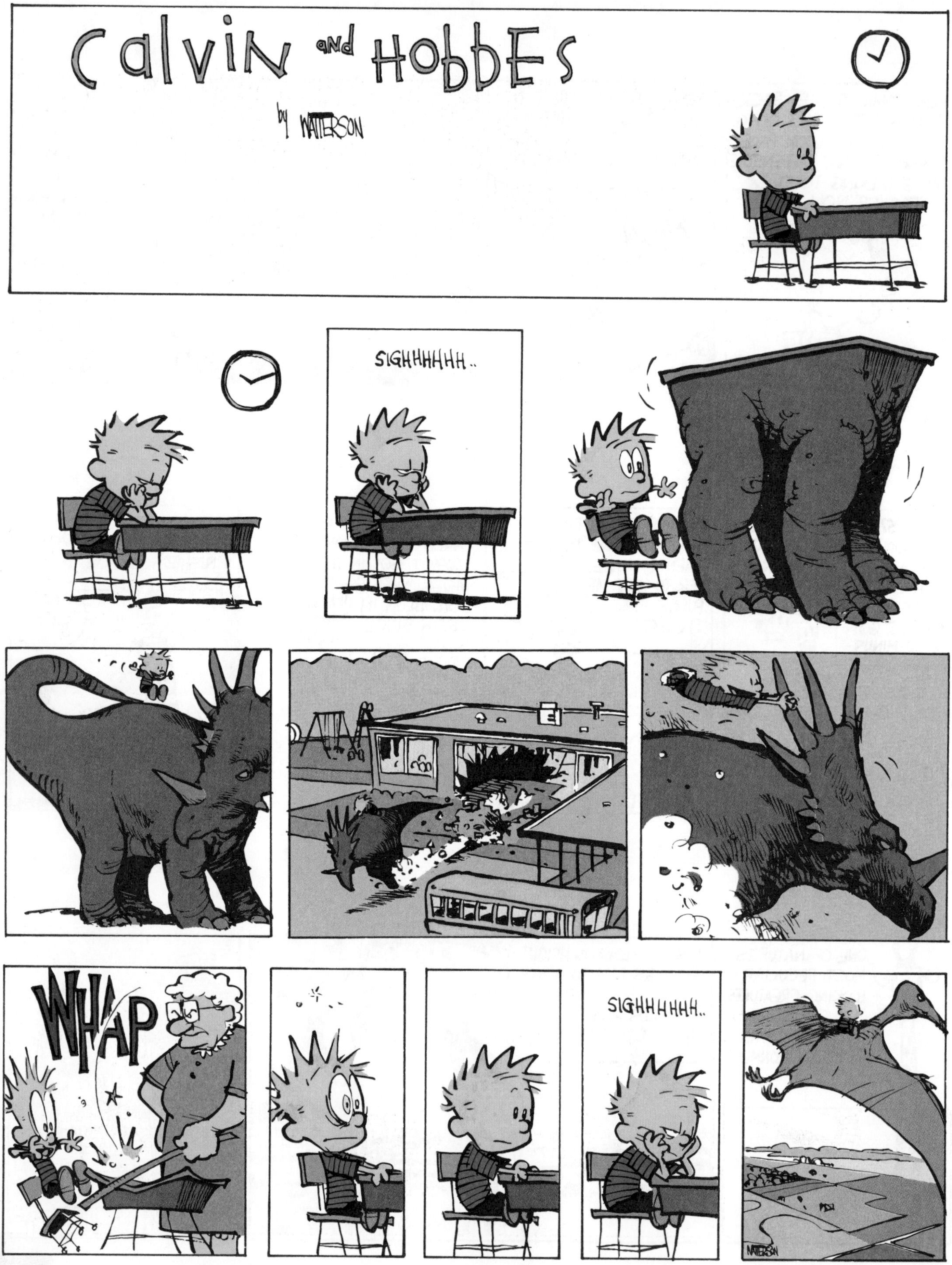
Calvin and HOBBES
by WATTERSON
SIGHHHHHH..
WHAP
SIGHHHHHH..
WATTERSON

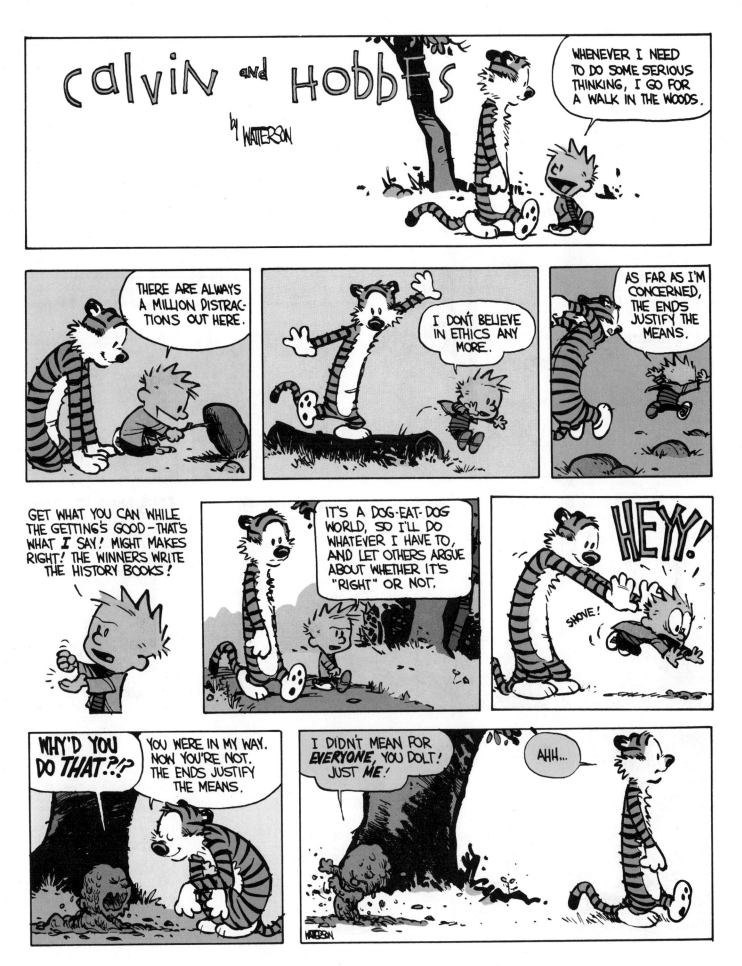

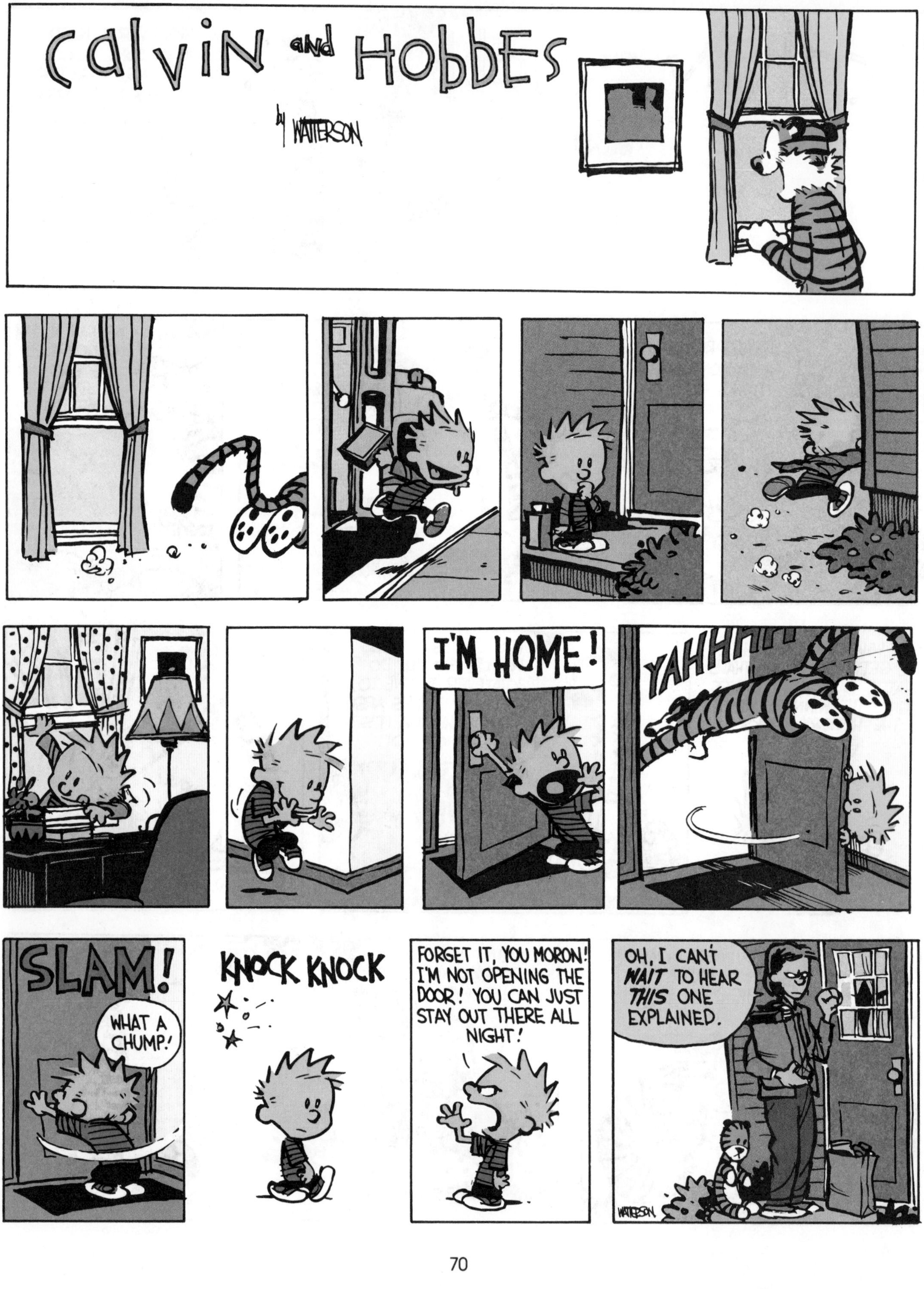
Calvin and HOBBES
by WATTERSON
I'M HOME!
YAHHHH
SLAM!
WHAT A CHUMP!
KNOCK KNOCK
FORGET IT, YOU MORON! I'M NOT OPENING THE DOOR! YOU CAN JUST STAY OUT THERE ALL NIGHT!
OH, I CAN'T *WAIT* TO HEAR *THIS* ONE EXPLAINED.
WATTERSON

74

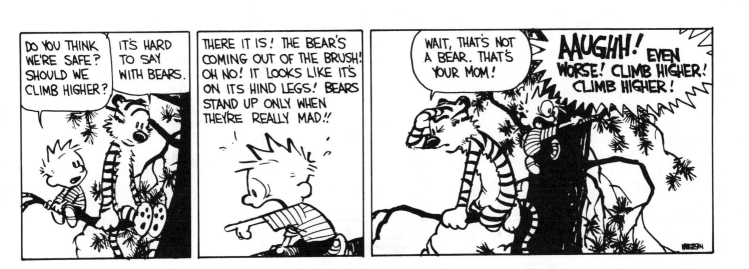

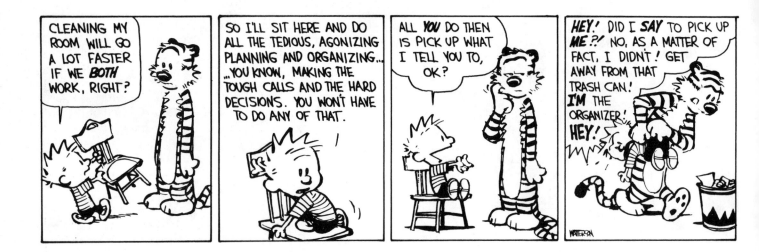

110

I PERFORMED A SCIENTIFIC EXPERIMENT TODAY.

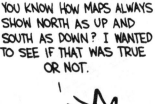

YOU KNOW HOW MAPS ALWAYS SHOW NORTH AS UP AND SOUTH AS DOWN? I WANTED TO SEE IF THAT WAS TRUE OR NOT.

WHAT DID YOU FIND OUT?

NOT MUCH. YOUR COMPASS DIDN'T SURVIVE THE TRIP SOUTH FROM THE TOP OF THE TREE.

MY COMPASS?!

LET ME KNOW WHEN YOU GET A NEW ONE. MY JUNIOR SCIENTIST BOOK SAYS NOT TO GET DISCOURAGED BY TEMPORARY SETBACKS.

I'VE BEEN THINKING. YOU KNOW HOW BORING DAD IS? MAYBE IT'S A BIG PHONY ACT!

MAYBE AFTER HE PUTS US TO BED, DAD DONS SOME WEIRD COSTUME AND GOES OUT FIGHTING CRIME! MAYBE THIS WHOLE "DAD" STUFF IS JUST A SECRET IDENTITY!

MAYBE THE MAYOR CALLS DAD ON A SECRET HOT LINE WHENEVER THE CITY'S IN TROUBLE! MAYBE DAD'S A MASKED SUPERHERO!

IF THAT'S TRUE HE SHOULD DRIVE A COOLER CAR.

I KNOW. OURS DOESN'T EVEN HAVE A CASSETTE DECK.

THERE'S THE STEGOSAURUS OUT FRONT! THERE'S THE NATURAL HISTORY MUSEUM! HOORAY!

I CAN'T WAIT TO SEE ALL THE DINOSAURS! C'MON, LET'S HURRY!

IT'S CERTAINLY BEEN A WHILE SINCE WE'VE BEEN HERE, HASN'T IT?

AT THE MUSEUM'S REQUEST, YES.

OH, THAT'S RIGHT, CALVIN, NO BITING PEOPLE THIS TIME, REMEMBER?

RROWRR

117

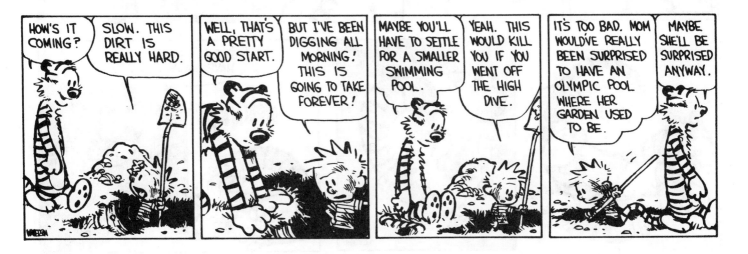

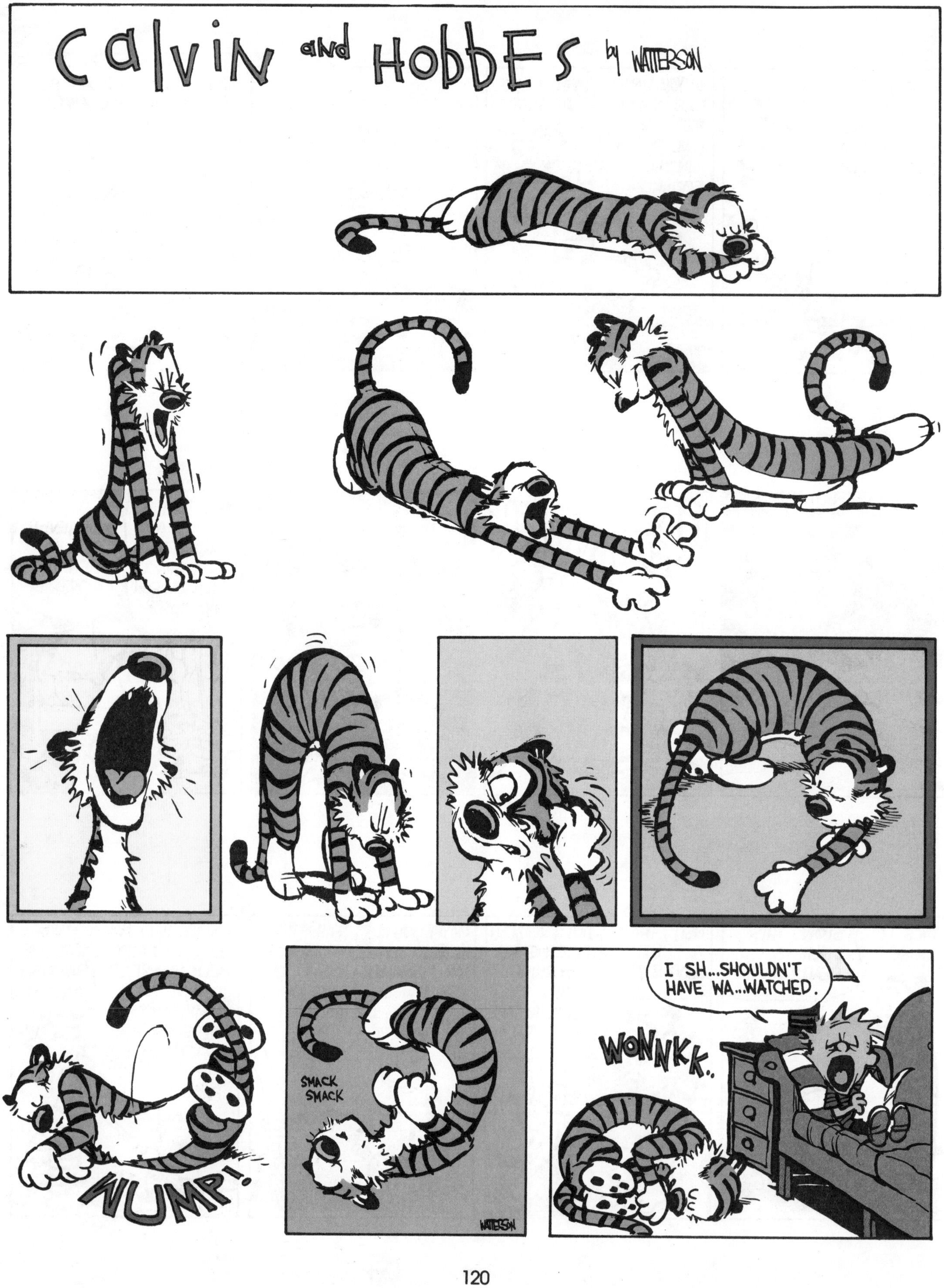
Calvin and HOBBES by WATTERSON
WUMP!
SMACK SMACK
WATTERSON
I SH...SHOULDN'T HAVE WA...WATCHED.
WONNKK..

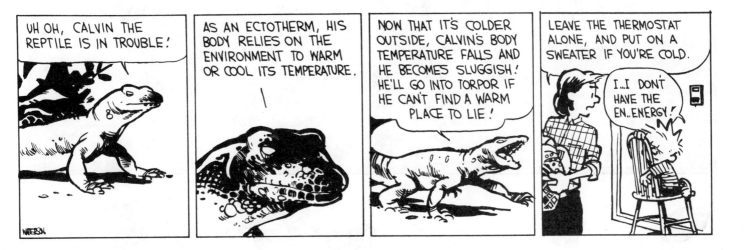

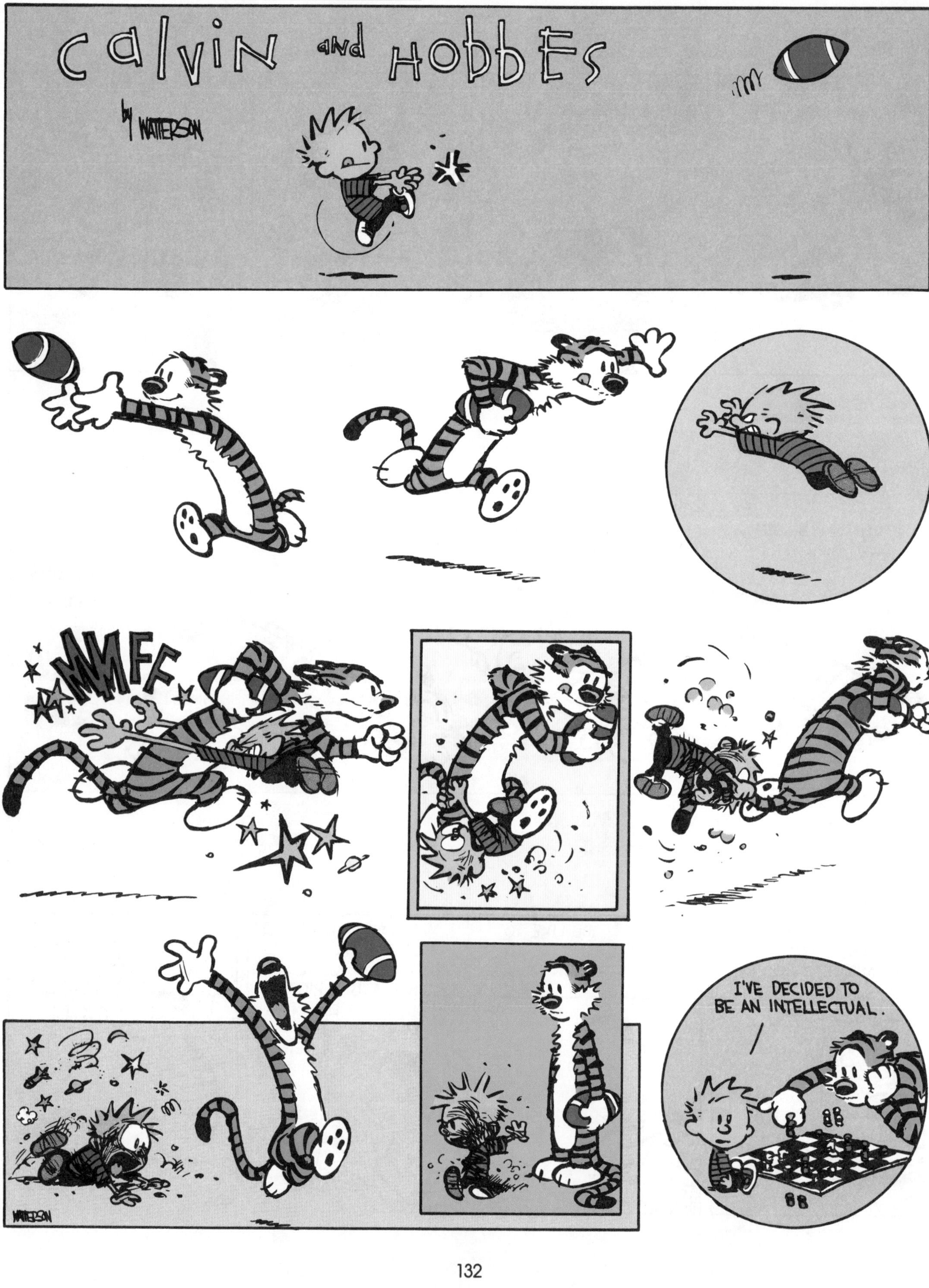
Calvin and Hobbes
by WATTERSON
MMFF
WATTERSON
I'VE DECIDED TO BE AN INTELLECTUAL.

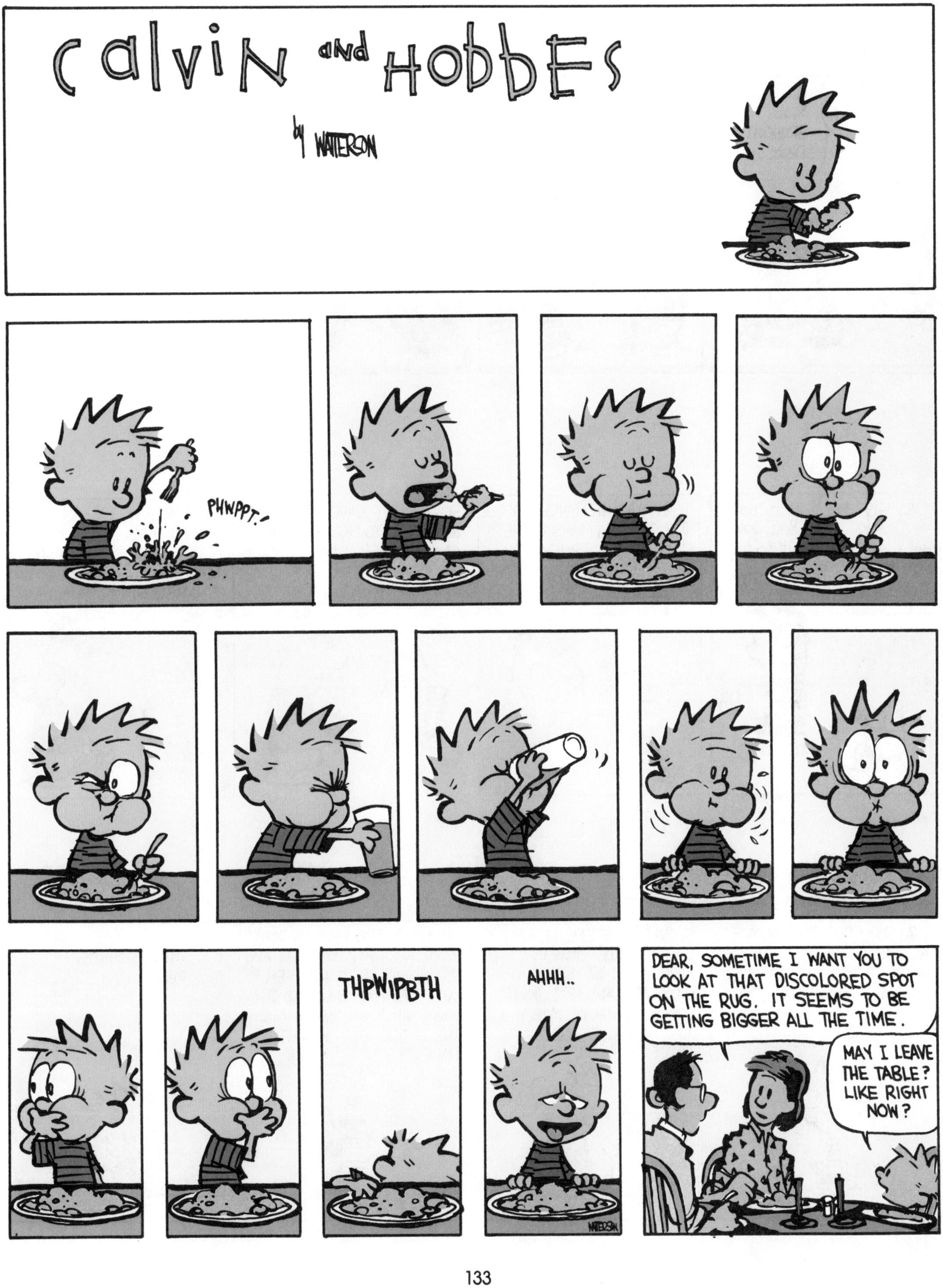
Calvin and HOBBES
by WATTERSON
PHWPPT!
THPWIPBTH
AHHH..
DEAR, SOMETIME I WANT YOU TO LOOK AT THAT DISCOLORED SPOT ON THE RUG. IT SEEMS TO BE GETTING BIGGER ALL THE TIME.
MAY I LEAVE THE TABLE? LIKE RIGHT NOW?
WATTERSON

BY GOLLY, I **AM** GOING TO STEAL MY TRUCK BACK FROM MOE! IT'S MINE AND HE HAS NO RIGHT TO HAVE IT!

I'LL JUST SNEAK UP BEHIND THE SWINGS HERE, AND WHEN MOE'S NOT LOOKING, I'LL RUN UP, GRAB THE TRUCK AND TAKE OFF!

THIS PLAYGROUND SHOULD HAVE ONE OF THOSE AUTOMATIC INSURANCE MACHINES LIKE THEY HAVE IN AIRPORTS.

OK, MOE'S GOT HIS BACK TO ME! NOW I'LL ZIP OVER, STEAL MY TRUCK BACK AND RUN LIKE CRAZY!

HE'LL NEVER KNOW WHAT HIT HIM! BY THE TIME HE SEES THE TRUCK IS GONE, I'LL BE A MILE AWAY! IT'S A FAIL-PROOF PLAN! NOTHING CAN GO WRONG! IT'S A SNAP!

THERE'S NO REASON TO HESITATE. IT'LL BE OVER IN A SPLIT SECOND, AND I'LL SURE BE GLAD TO HAVE MY TRUCK BACK! I'LL JUST DO IT AND BE DONE! NOTHING TO IT! IT'S EASY!

OBVIOUSLY MY BODY DOESN'T BELIEVE A WORD MY BRAIN IS SAYING.

PHOOEY, WHO AM I KIDDING? I'D NEVER GET AWAY WITH STEALING MY TRUCK BACK FROM MOE. THE UGLY GALOOT IS THE SIZE OF A BUICK.

HMM... SINCE I CAN'T **FIGHT** HIM, MAYBE I SHOULD TRY **TALKING** TO HIM. MAYBE IF I REASONED WITH HIM, HE'D SEE **MY** SIDE.

MAYBE HE'D REALIZE THAT STEALING HURTS PEOPLE, AND MAYBE HE'D RETURN MY TRUCK **WILLINGLY**.

MAYBE IF I'M REALLY LUCKY I WON'T GO THROUGH LIFE WITH THE NICKNAME "OMELET FACE."

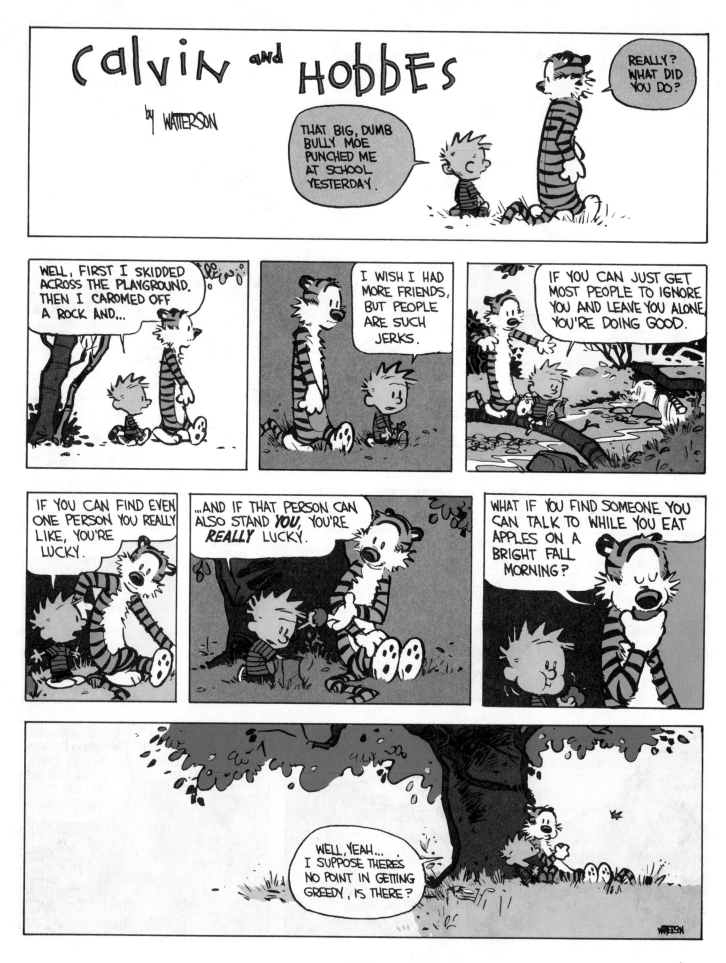

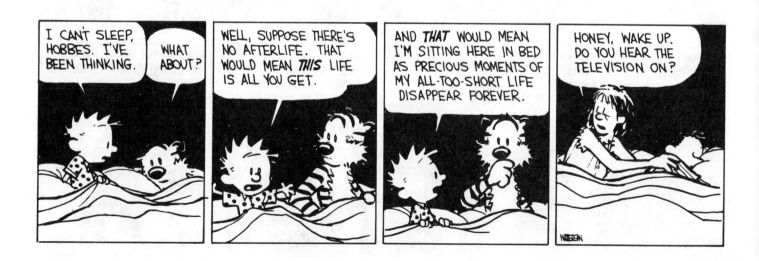

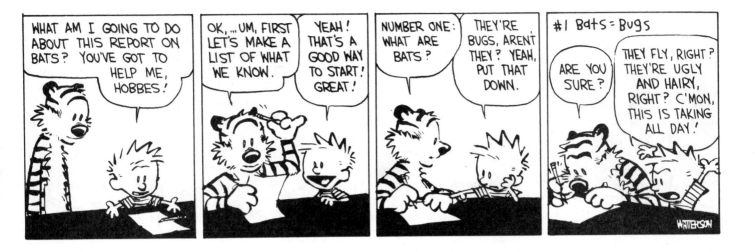

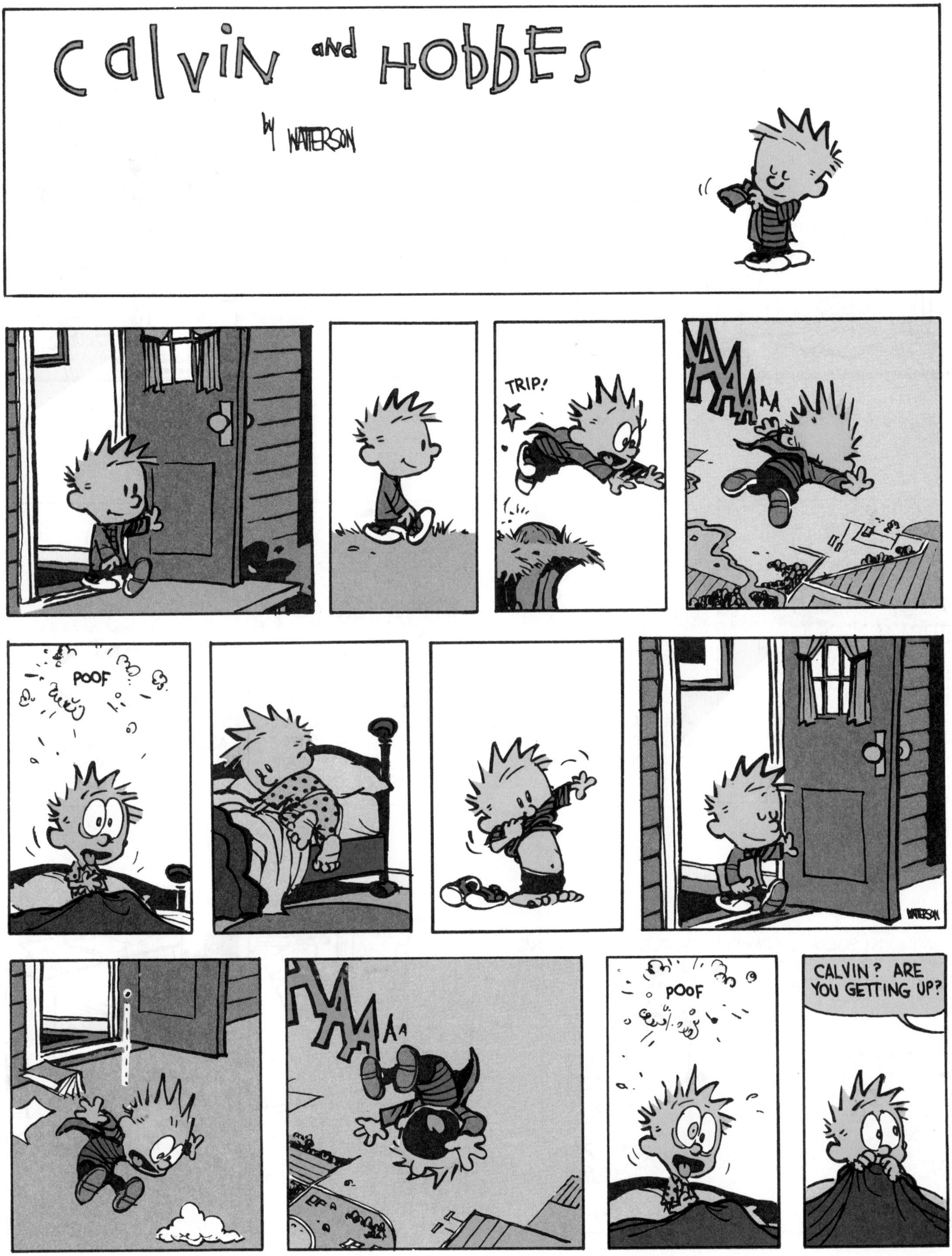
Calvin and HOBBES
by WATTERSON
TRIP!
AAAAAA
POOF
WATTERSON
AAAA
POOF
CALVIN? ARE YOU GETTING UP?

MOM AND DAD WON'T BE TOO HAPPY ABOUT *THIS*. NO SIR.

DAD WILL HAVE TO BOLT MY BED TO THE CEILING TONIGHT, AND MOM WILL HAVE TO STAND ON A STEPLADDER TO HAND ME DINNER.

THEN I'LL HAVE TO HOLD MY PLATE UPSIDE-DOWN ABOVE MY HEAD AND SCRAPE THE FOOD OFF THE UNDERSIDE! AND IF I SPILL ANYTHING, IT WILL FLY 10 FEET UP TO THE FLOOR AND SPLOT!

THIS IS GOING TO BE THE MOST FUN I'VE EVER HAD!

ALL THIS WIDE OPEN CEILING SPACE! I WISH I COULD GET MY ROLLER SKATES.

HEY, MAYBE I CAN CLIMB UP THIS BOOKCASE AND WHEN I GET TO THE BOTTOM SHELF, LEAP TO A CHAIR!

THEN I CAN PULL MYSELF ACROSS TO OTHER PIECES OF FURNITURE AND WORK MY WAY TO MY TOY CHEST.

...I CAN HEAR MOM NOW: "HOW ON EARTH DID YOU GET SNEAKER PRINTS ON THE UNDERSIDE OF EACH SHELF?!"

THERE! I THINK I CAN JUMP TO THAT CHAIR AND HANG ONTO THE BACK.

GEERONIMOOO!

¡WHOAAA!

WHAM!

GREAT. JUST GREAT.

CALVIN, QUIT BANGING AROUND!

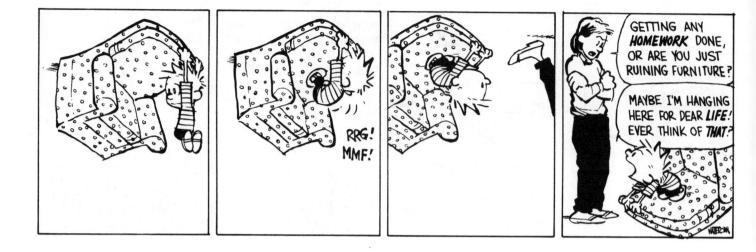

Christmas Eve

ON WINDOW PANES, THE ICY FROST
LEAVES FEATHERED PATTERNS, CRISSED & CROSSED,
BUT IN OUR HOUSE THE CHRISTMAS TREE
IS DECORATED FESTIVELY
WITH TINY DOTS OF COLORED LIGHT
THAT COZY UP THIS WINTER NIGHT.
CHRISTMAS SONGS, FAMILIAR, SLOW,
PLAY SOFTLY ON THE RADIO.
POPS AND HISSES FROM THE FIRE
WHISTLE WITH THE BELLS AND CHOIR.
MY TIGER IS NOW FAST ASLEEP
ON HIS BACK AND DREAMING DEEP.
WHEN THE FIRE MAKES HIM HOT,
HE TURNS TO WARM WHATEVER'S NOT.
PROPPED AGAINST HIM ON THE RUG,
I GIVE MY FRIEND A GENTLE HUG.
TOMORROW'S WHAT I'M WAITING FOR,
BUT I CAN WAIT A LITTLE MORE.

calvin and HOBBES
by WATTERSON

ARE YOU KIDDING?

ARE YOUR PARENTS GOING OUT FOR NEW YEAR'S EVE?

MY PARENTS' IDEA OF A WILD NIGHT IS TO MIX A SCOOP OF REAL COFFEE IN WITH THE DECAF.

ARE YOU MAKING ANY RESOLUTIONS FOR THE NEW YEAR?

RESOLUTIONS? **ME**?? JUST WHAT ARE YOU IMPLYING? THAT I NEED TO **CHANGE**?? WELL, BUDDY, AS FAR AS **I'M** CONCERNED, I'M PERFECT THE WAY I AM!

FOR YOUR INFORMATION, I'M **STAYING** LIKE THIS, AND EVERYONE ELSE CAN JUST GET **USED** TO IT! IF PEOPLE DON'T LIKE ME THE WAY I AM, WELL, **TOUGH** BEANS! IT'S A FREE COUNTRY! I DON'T NEED ANYONE'S PERMISSION TO BE THE WAY I WANT! THIS IS HOW I AM - TAKE IT OR LEAVE IT!

BY GOLLY, LIFE'S TOO DARN SHORT TO WASTE TIME TRYING TO PLEASE EVERY MEDDLESOME MORON WHO'S GOT AN IDEA HOW I OUGHT TO BE! I DON'T NEED ADVICE! EVERYONE CAN JUST STAY OUT OF MY FACE!

I...

.."HOBBES?

HMPH!

HE SHOULD RESOLVE TO BE MORE ATTENTIVE WHEN SOMEONE IS SPEAKING.

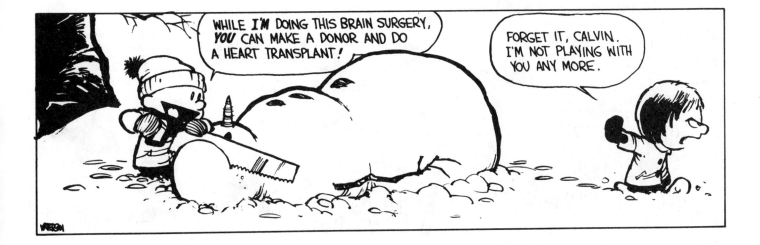

Panel 1: OK DUPLICATES, LISTEN UP. AS LONG AS YOU'RE ALL HERE AND I DON'T KNOW HOW TO GET RID OF YOU, WE MIGHT AS WELL COOPERATE.

Panel 2: SPECIFICALLY, WITH FIVE DUPLICATES, WE CAN DIVIDE UP THE SCHOOL WEEK SO THERE'S ONE DUPLICATE FOR EACH DAY.

Panel 3: IF THE REST OF US LAY LOW, WE CAN TAKE TURNS GOING TO SCHOOL, AND NO ONE WILL BE THE WISER!

GREAT!

Panel 4: NOW THAT STILL LEAVES US WITH THE QUESTION OF WHO GETS THE BED TONIGHT.

WE'LL FIGHT YOU FOR IT.

Panel 5: HI CALVIN.

I'M NOT CALVIN. I'M DUPLICATE NUMBER TWO.

Panel 6: WHAT ARE YOU TALKING ABOUT?

WE DREW STRAWS, AND TODAY'S MY DAY TO GO TO SCHOOL. WE'RE ALL TAKING TURNS SO WE EACH ONLY GO ONCE A WEEK.

Panel 7: CALVIN, YOU ARE SO WEIRD I'M NOT EVEN GOING TO TALK TO YOU.

I'M NOT CALVIN.

Panel 8: I WISH I LIVED SOMEPLACE WHERE I WENT TO A NORMAL BUS STOP.

ARE YOU IN CALVIN'S CLASS? WILL YOU HELP ME FIND HIS LOCKER?

Panel 9: CALVIN, WOULD YOU PLEASE DEMONSTRATE THE HOMEWORK PROBLEM YOU WERE ASSIGNED YESTERDAY?

Panel 10: I WASN'T HERE YESTERDAY.

YES, YOU WERE, CALVIN. DIDN'T YOU DO YOUR PROBLEM?

Panel 11: I'M NOT CALVIN. I'M DUPLICATE NUMBER FIVE. DUPLICATE *TWO* WAS HERE YESTERDAY, NOT *ME*. WE'RE ALL TAKING TURNS. NUMBER TWO WILL BE BACK NEXT WEEK, AND YOU CAN ASK HIM TO DO THE PROBLEM *THEN*.

Panel 12: LOOK, I DON'T SEE WHAT'S SO HARD ABOUT THIS!

PRINCIPAL

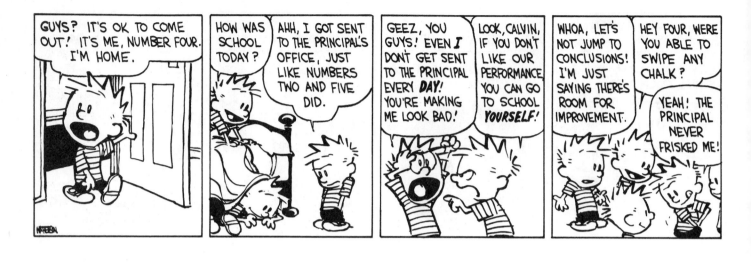

QUIZ:
Jack and Joe leave their homes at the same time and drive toward each other. Jack drives at 60 mph, while Joe drives at 30 mph. They pass each other in 10 minutes.

How far apart were Jack and Joe when they started?

IT WAS ANOTHER BAFFLING CASE. BUT THEN, YOU DON'T HIRE A **PRIVATE EYE** FOR THE **EASY** ONES...

I'D PLANNED TO TAKE THE DAY **OFF** AND SPEND TIME WITH A COUPLE OF **BUDDIES**. MY BUDDIES TRAVEL LIGHT AND THEY'RE FUN TO HAVE AROUND. ONE TRAVELS IN A HOLSTER, AND THE OTHER IN A HIP FLASK.

MY NAME IS **BULLET**. TRACER BULLET. WHAT PEOPLE **CALL** ME IS SOMETHING ELSE AGAIN. I'M A PRIVATE EYE. IT SAYS SO ON MY DOOR.

THE **LAST** THING I WANTED THIS MORNING WAS A **CASE** TO SOLVE, BUT THE DAME WHO BROUGHT IT WAS **PERSUASIVE**. MOST DAMES **ARE**, SOMEHOW.

GET TO WORK, CALVIN.

I TOLD HER IT WOULD COST HER FIFTY GREENBACKS A DAY, PLUS EXPENSES.

I STEPPED OUT INTO THE RAINY STREETS AND REVIEWED THE FACTS. THERE WEREN'T MANY.

TWO SAPS, JACK AND JOE, DRIVE TOWARD EACH OTHER AT 60 AND 30 MPH. AFTER 10 MINUTES, THEY PASS. I'M SUPPOSED TO FIND OUT HOW FAR APART THEY STARTED.

QUESTIONS POUR DOWN LIKE THE RAIN. WHO **ARE** THESE MUGS? WHAT WERE THEY TRYING TO ACCOMPLISH? WHY WAS JACK IN SUCH A HURRY? AND WHAT DIFFERENCE DOES IT MAKE WHERE THEY STARTED FROM??

I HAD A HUNCH THAT, BEFORE THIS WAS OVER, I'D BE SORRY I ASKED.

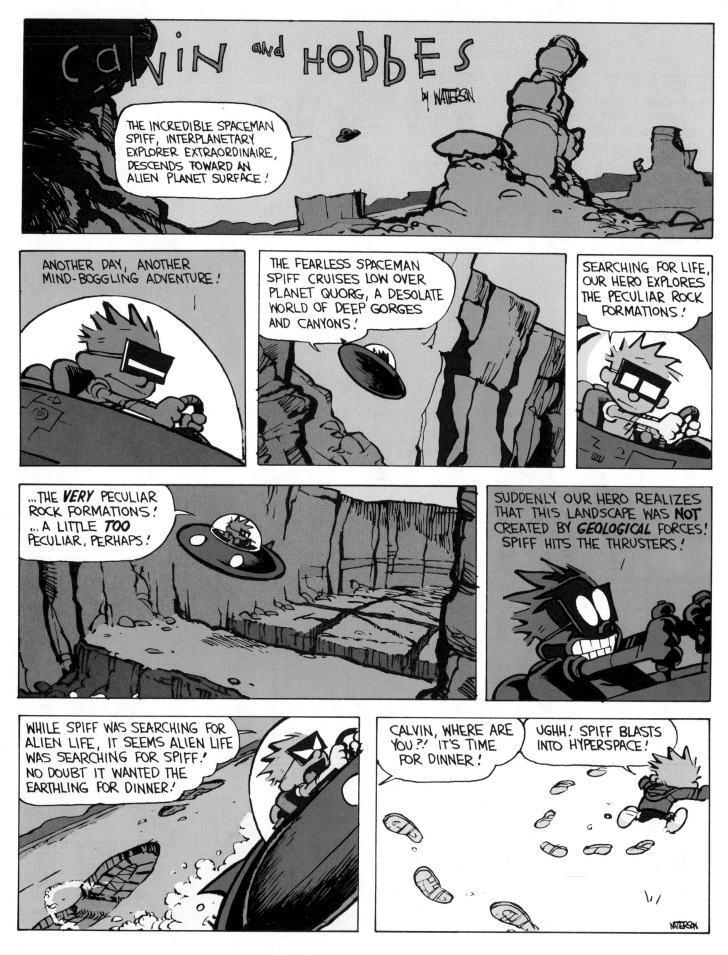

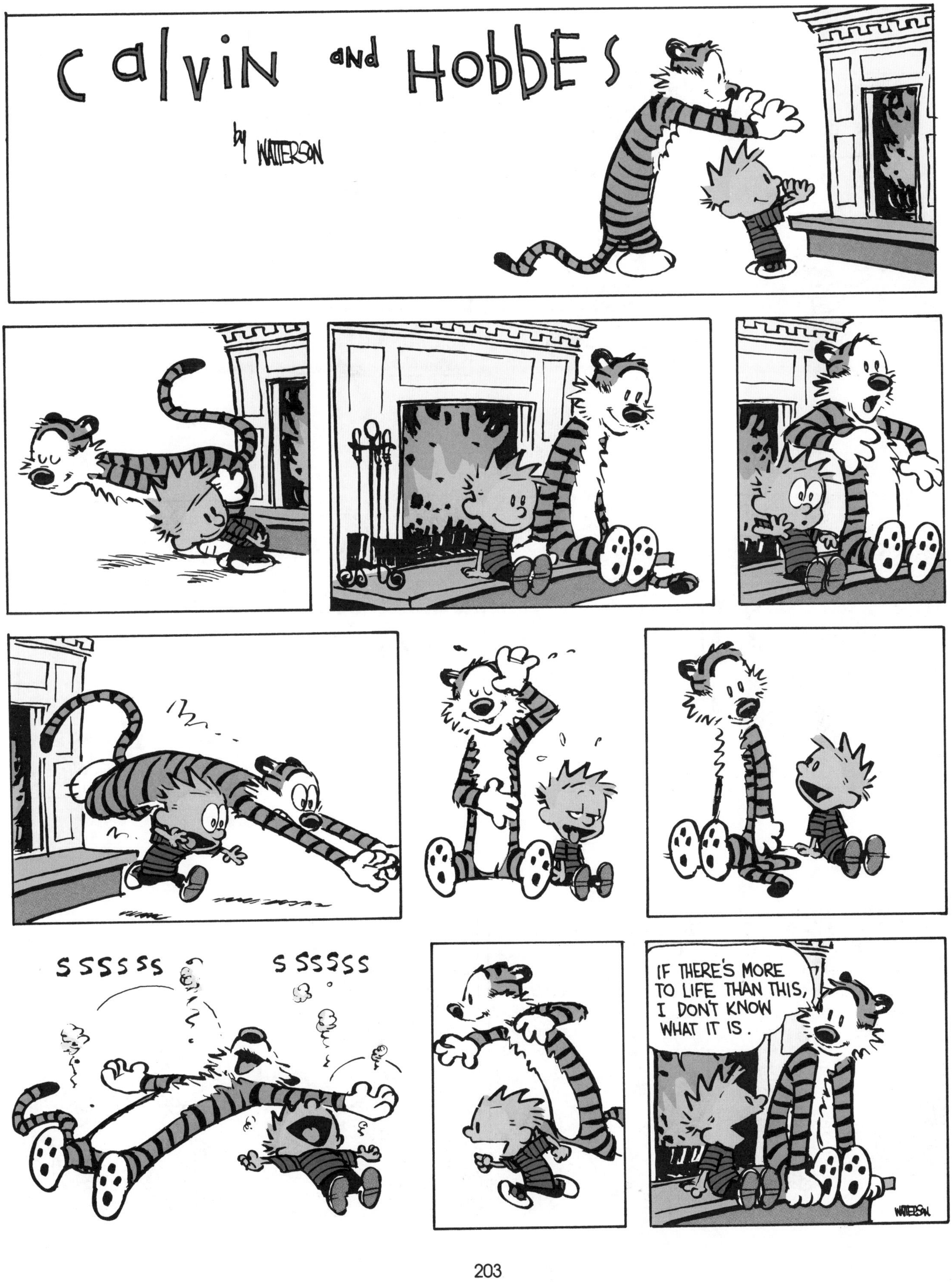
Calvin and HOBBES
by WATTERSON
SSSSSS
SSSSSS
IF THERE'S MORE TO LIFE THAN THIS, I DON'T KNOW WHAT IT IS.
WATTERSON

957.

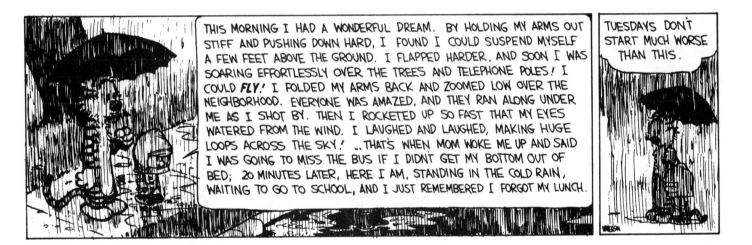

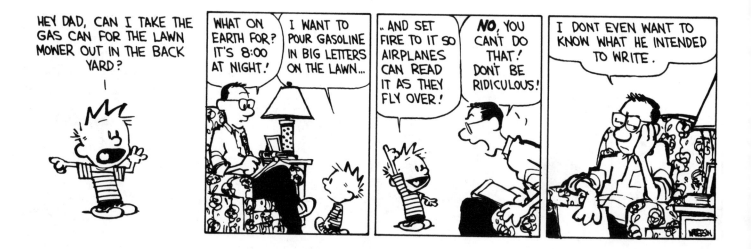

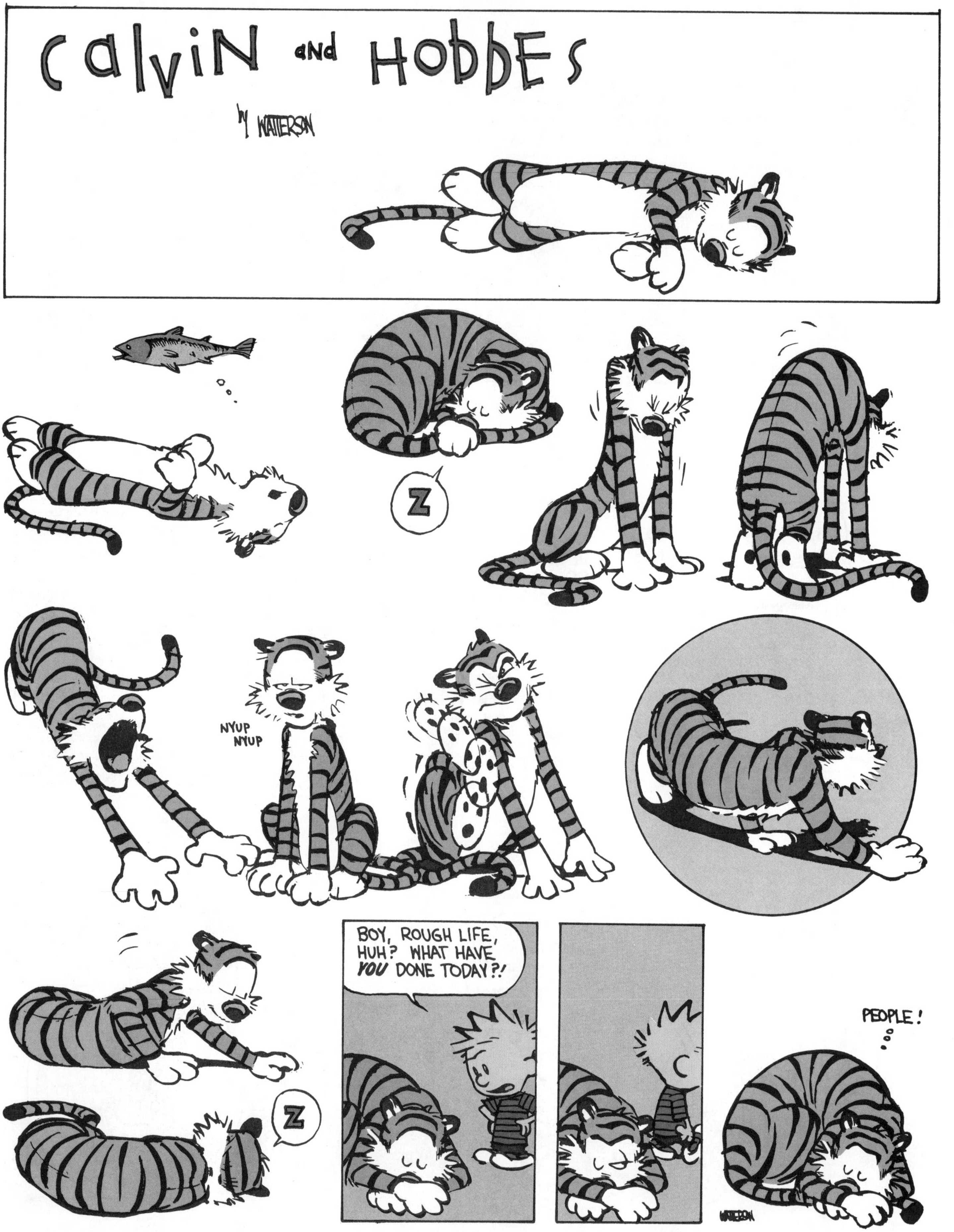
Calvin and HOBBES
by WATTERSON
Z
NYUP NYUP
Z
BOY, ROUGH LIFE, HUH? WHAT HAVE *YOU* DONE TODAY?!
PEOPLE!
WATTERSON

216

224

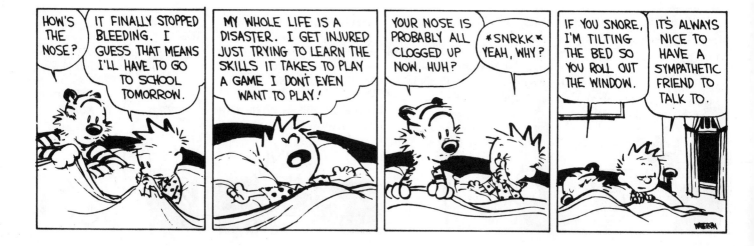

235

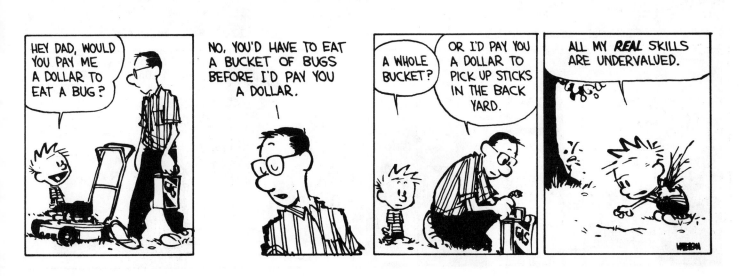

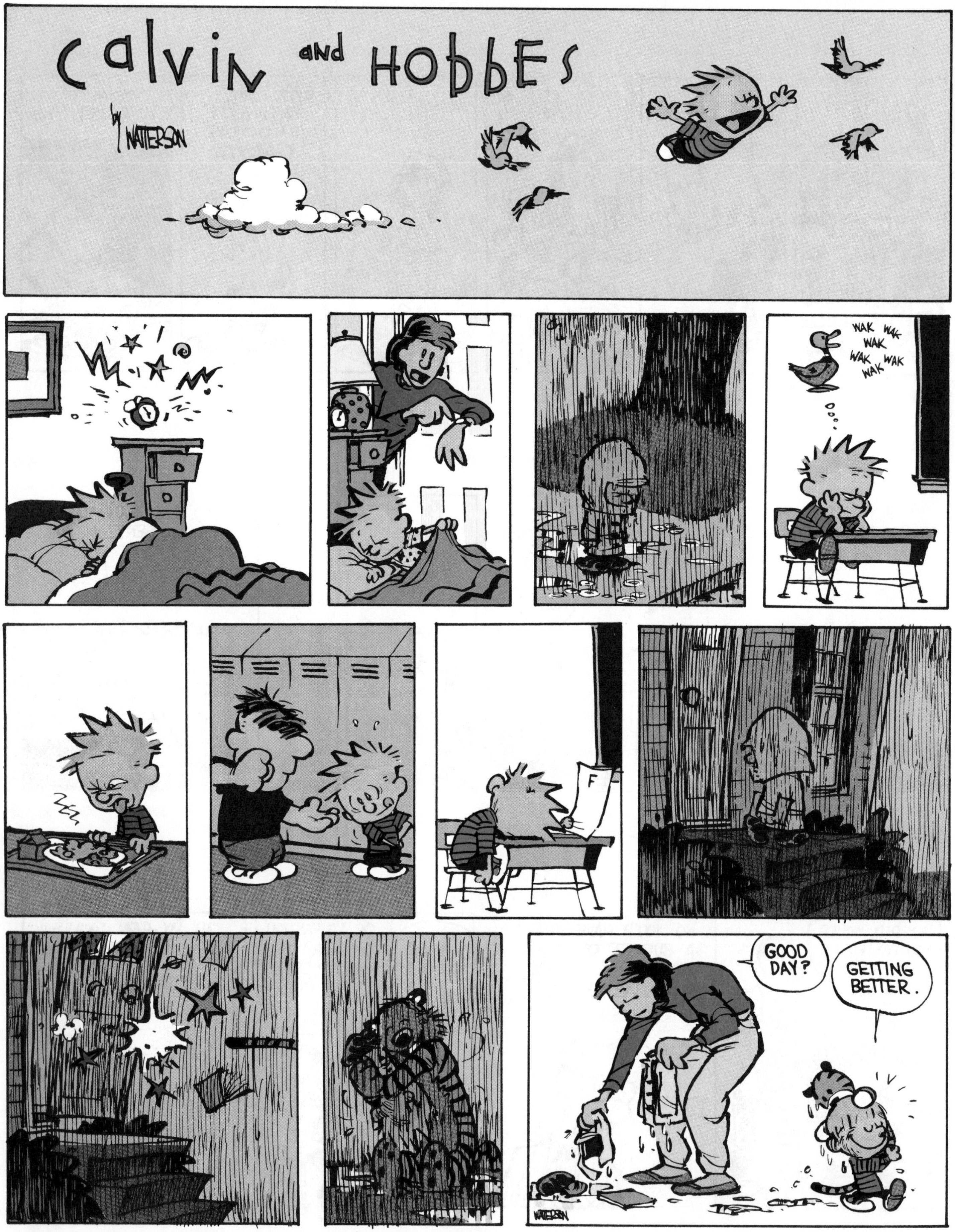
Calvin and HOBBES
by WATTERSON
WAK WAK WAK WAK WAK WAK
F
GOOD DAY?
GETTING BETTER.
WATTERSON

ON DISTANT PLANET ZARK, WE FIND THE EMPTY RED SPACECRAFT OF OUR HERO, THE BOLD *SPACEMAN SPIFF!*

UH OH! UP AHEAD, THE ROCKS ARE CHARRED WITH DEATH RAY BLASTS! A VIOLENT STRUGGLE TOOK PLACE HERE!

AND ONLY THE TRACKS OF A LARGE, SINISTER ALIEN LEAVE THE SCENE! WHAT HAS HAPPENED TO THE EARTHLING EXPLORER?

CALVIN, THIS IS HUMILIATING!!

I DON'T WANT TO GO! PUT ME DOWN!

SPACEMAN SPIFF IS BEING HELD PRISONER BY HIDEOUS ALIENS! WHAT DO THEY WANT WITH HIM?

SPIFF IS SOON TO FIND OUT! OUR HERO IS CALLED BEFORE THE ALIEN POTENTATE!

..WHERE IT BECOMES CLEAR THAT SPIFF IS ABOUT TO BE *SACRIFICED*...

..TO APPEASE THE EVIL GOD THEY CALL "NOLLIJ"!

UP TO THE BLACKBOARD. HURRY UP.

STARING DEATH IN THE FACE, OUR HERO THINKS FAST.

$11 - 4 =$

INCHING CLOSER TO THE SACRIFICIAL PIT, SPIFF SLOWLY AND SMOOTHLY REACHES FOR THE TINY ATOM BLASTER CONCEALED IN HIS BELT!

YAA! ALL RIGHT, YOU BLOODSUCKING, MUTANT CHROMOSOMAL DISASTERS! NOBODY MOVE! I'M OUTTA HERE!

CALVIN, GIVE ME THAT RUBBER BAND RIGHT THIS MINUTE!

I SAID NOBODY MOVE!

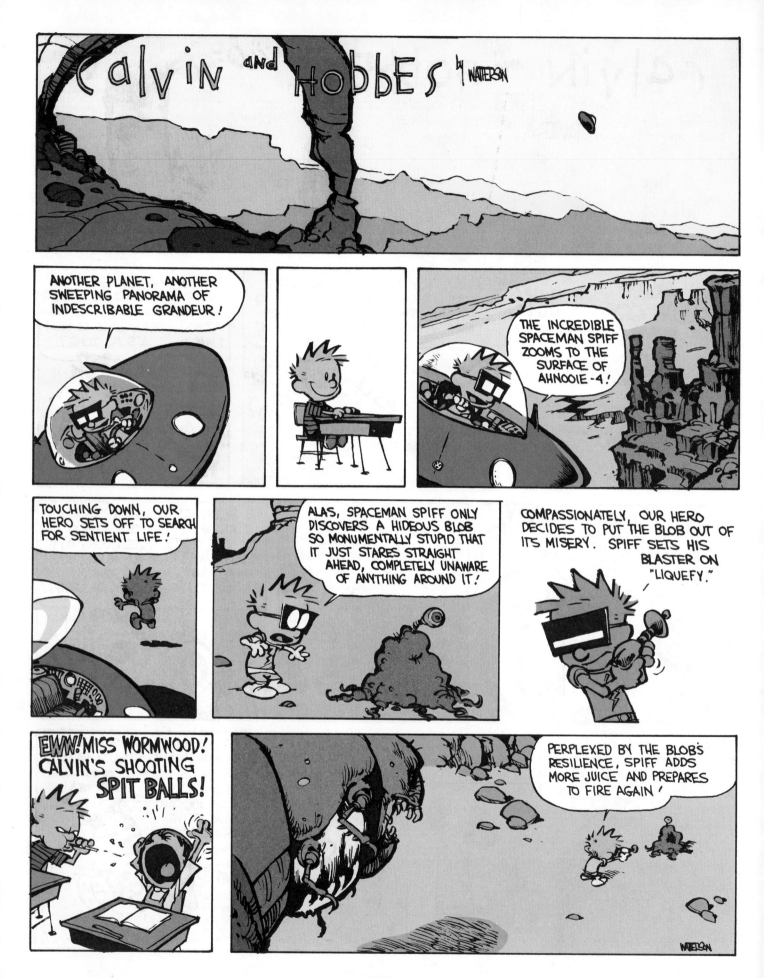

247

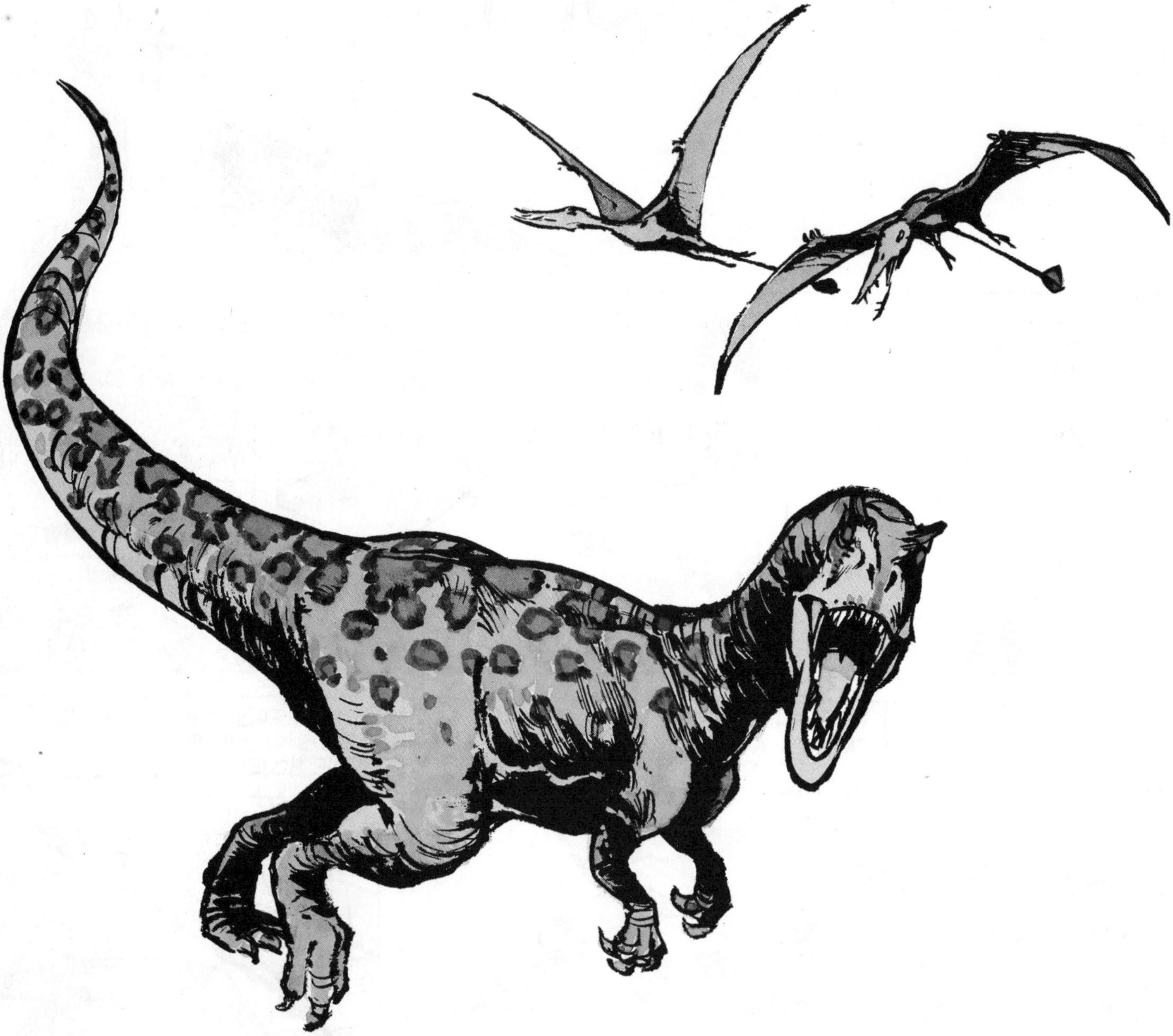

The End